The Daily Companion
Volume 3

The Daily Companion
Volume 3

Compiled by
Elizabeth Rundle

Collins

Marshall Pickering

William Collins Sons & Co. Ltd
London • Glasgow • Sydney • Auckland
Toronto • Johannesburg

First published in Great Britain in 1990 by Marshall Pickering

Marshall Pickering is an imprint of
Collins Religious Division,
part of the Collins Publishing Group
8 Grafton Street, London W1X 3LA

Printed and bound in Great Britain by William Collins Sons &
Co. Ltd, Glasgow

Typeset by Burns & Smith Ltd, Derby

CONDITIONS OF SALE

1st January

Here I am! I stand at the door and knock. If anyone hears
my voice and opens the door, I will go in...

Revelation 3:20

Happy New Year! As the midnight hour strikes, everybody
wishes everybody else this 'happiness' – it fills the air like
some great universal, heart-felt song. I looked up the word
'happy' in one of the dictionaries and it read: 'in secure
possession of good... blessed... living peacably together'.

Lord, what a Happy New Year it could be if each heart
knew the blessedness of living peacably together, secure in
the certain knowledge of the grace of our Lord Jesus Christ.
As I set my eyes once more into the unknown of another year
I pause to pray... to listen to Your voice... I open my heart
again to my Saviour... Bless me, Lord, love me and guide
me in every new moment.

> *Standing at the portal of the opening year,*
> *Words of comfort meet us, hushing every fear;*
> *Spoken through the silence by our Father's voice*
> *Tender, strong and faithful, making us rejoice!*
> *God is all-sufficient for the coming year.*
>
> *Francis Ridley Havergal*

*   *   *

2nd January

In Him was life, and that life was the light of men.

John 1:4

> *Father, I believe that You are Light*
> *and in You there is no darkness at all.*
> *I believe that You are Love*
> *and in You there is no hatred or revenge.*
> *Your love was shown to us*
> *when You made us Your children in Jesus Christ.*
> *When His face shines upon us*

1

we know the darkness is passing away
and the Light is already shining.
Father, whoever says he is in light and hates his brother
is, for all his eloquence, still in darkness.
It is the man who cares for his brother
who is living in Light.
Such a one will never stumble or lose his way,
for the darkness has been lifted from his eyes...

B. P. B.

Lord, help me not to stumble over dark emotions... bring Your Light into my new year... enable me to love with Your Love so that each new day may be lived to Your glory.

* * *

3rd January

They (some Pharisees and Herodians) came to Jesus and said: 'Teacher, we know you are a man of integrity... you teach the way of God in accordance with the truth.'

Mark 12:14

This is truly an enlightening passage. With their words these leaders of Judaism were honouring Jesus for his integrity, they were acknowledging that He taught God's word of truth, and yet their hearts were so frozen that they were merely out to trap Him. From our standpoint it seems quite incredible that men of such learning and intellect could do anything other than become followers of Jesus, but it is sadly obvious that their only motive was to ensnare Jesus with their own wisdom.

When I stop to think about it, Lord, the same attitudes are in evidence today – people of great learning are better inclined to argue with Christian teaching than place their faith in the bleeding hands of Jesus their Saviour. Lord, the more I know, the more I realize I don't know anything... I know that You know everything, and that is enough to carry me through this day. May others see that 'knowing' is not half so important as trusting and caring.

People don't care how much we know until they know how much we care.

Floyd McClung

*   *   *

4th January

The sound of rejoicing in Jerusalem could be heard far away.

Nehemiah 12:43

The elaborate celebrations for dedicating the wall of Jerusalem are vividly portrayed in the book of Nehemia. A huge crowd gathered, singers came in from surrounding villages to form two choirs, there were the obligatory officials, priests, instrumentalists, women and children... quite a day out! The whole nation was united in praise and thanksgiving to God and their rejoicing was plain for all to see and hear.

I know, Lord, that we cannot constantly be in the euphoria of splendid celebrations, but I pray that if anything in my life is plain for all to see and hear, then let it be my rejoicing and not by bouts of dissatisfaction. When I'm on the verge of a grumble I will think of a happy hymn or song and repeat the uplifting words... The sound of rejoicing will at least carry from my lips to my heart!

Rejoice in the Lord always, and again I say rejoice.

Philippians 4:4

*   *   *

5th January

Take to heart all the words I have solemnly declared to you this day... They are not just idle words for you – they are your life.

Deuteronomy 32:46–47

We are all so good with words – there are endless talks,

discussion groups, training committees, and mountains of words being erected as it were. Oh, I know that often they are pious words, Biblical words, theological words, erudite words, but they are still only words... There was a wonderful Christian lady in my last church. She came from the West Indies. She was not especially articulate and she will live and die without speaking in public, but she could and did tell me more about her Saviour not with her lips but far, far more with her life. What are you saying with your life?

The Rev. John Jackson

Take my life and let it be consecrated, Lord, to Thee:
Take my moments and my days; let them flow in ceaseless praise.

Francis Ridley Havergall

*   *   *

6th January

Now the earth was corrupt in God's sight and was full of violence. God saw how corrupt the earth had become, for all the people on earth had corrupted their ways. So God said to Noah: 'I am going to put an end to all people, for the earth is filled with violence because of them. I am surely going to destroy both them and the earth. So make yourself an ark...' Noah did everything just as God commanded him.

The Lord then said to Noah, 'Go into the ark, you and your whole family, because I have found you righteous in this generation. Take with you seven of every kind of clean animal, a male and its mate, and two of every kind of unclean animal, a male and its mate, and also seven of every kind of bird, male and female, to keep their various kinds alive throughout the earth. Seven days from now I will send rain on the earth for forty days and forty nights, and I will wipe from the face of the earth every living creature I have made.'

And Noah did all that the Lord commanded him.

Genesis 6:11–14, 22; 7:1–4

*   *   *

7th January

Jesus said: Whoever serves me must follow me.'

John 12:26

Say 'yes' son,
   I need your 'yes' as I needed Mary's 'yes' to come to earth, for it is I who must do your work: it is I who must live in your family; it is I who must be in your neighbourhood, and not you.
   Give all to me. Abandon all to me.
   I need your 'yes' to be united with you and to come down to earth –
   I need your 'yes' to continue saving the world!

Michel Quoist

Then let the servant Church arise,
A caring Church that longs to be
A partner in Christ's sacrifice,
And clothed in Christ's humility.
We have no mission but to serve
In full obedience to our Lord:
To care for all without reserve
And spread His liberating word.

F. Pratt Green

* * *

8th January

Jesus said: 'When you pray, go into your room, close the door and pray to your Father, who is unseen.'

Matthew 6:6

The jovial broadcaster Roger Royle once received from a listener a letter about the deep insights into things unseen which her daughter had had when she was a small child. Evidently on their shopping trips into the city, the mother always spent a few minutes in prayer in one of the churches. She explained to her daughter that they were visiting God's

5

house. After a few of these visits to an 'empty' church, the little girl enquired,: 'Why is God always out when we call?' Before her mother could think of a suitable reply her daughter answered her own question with extreme logic: 'I expect,' she decided, as if stating the obvious, 'He does His shopping the same time as we do.'

Thank you, Lord, for the trust of little children... Give me that childlike, praying trust today and every day.

Now faith is being sure of what we hope for and certain of what we do not see... Let us fix our eyes on Jesus, the author and perfector of our faith...

Hebrews 11:1; 12:2

* * *

9th January

After John the Baptist was put into prison, Jesus went into Galilee, proclaiming the good news of God. 'The time has come,' He said. 'The Kingdom of God is near.'

Mark 1:14

In his book *Radical Jesus*, Rev Dr John Vincent, President of the Methodist Conference 1989/90, has written: 'Christ's way of mission seems to me to involve very specific aspects, which give rise to strategies and methods. I would list the characteristics of Jesus' mission in Mark's gospel as setting out the areas and perspective for mission in Christ's way today: acting out radical happenings... announcing a radical manifesto... bringing liberation from bondage... giving power to the people... achieving solidarity with the poor... holding out welcome to forgiveness... exposing the politics of religion and State... embodying a counter-politics of the Kingdom. Let's support each other as we today set out our frail commitments in new embodiments of Christ and His radical practice of God's mission in the world.'

Lord, I pray for all those who today are bringing the light of Your love into the lives of people in need – the homeless, people in debt, prisoners of conscience, my brothers and sisters in degrading refugee camps… May Your good news of justice, love and peace be heard in the darkest places.

*   *   *

10th January

Cast all your anxiety on Him because He cares for you.

1 Peter 5:7

For the children the novelty stage of those carefully wrapped Christmas presents is now passed. When I look at what has been given to me I know that the gift itself is not that important, but what is of supreme importance is the love behind the gift. In fact, if I thought about approaching the manger with a gift I just don't know what I could give except my love. There is, after all, nothing my Lord wants except my love… The Lord of all gave Himself in love for my sake… To echo the words of the poet Christina Rossetti: What can I give him, poor as I am? Yet what I can I give Him – I give my heart.

O Lord, whose way is perfect, help us, we pray Thee, always to trust in Thy goodness: that, walking with Thee and following Thee in all simplicity we may possess quiet and contented minds, and may cast all our care on Thee, for Thou carest for us.

Christina Rossetti

*   *   *

11th January

Jesus answered: 'It is written, "Man does not live by bread alone but on every word that comes from the mouth of God." '

Matthew 4:4

Your words to me are life and health;
They fortify my soul,
Enable, guide and teach my heart

7

To reach its perfect goal.

Your words to me are light and truth;
From day to day they show
Their wisdom, passing earthly lore,
As in their truth I grow.

Your words to me are full of joy,
Of beauty, peace and grace,
From them I learn Your blessed will,
Through them I see Your face.

Your words are perfected in One,
Yourself, the Living Word;
Within my heart Your image print
In clearest lines, O Lord.

George C. Martin

Jesus said: 'Heaven and earth will pass away, but my words will never pass away.'

Mark 13:31

* * *

12th January

While they were there, the time came for the baby to be born, and she gave birth to her firstborn, a son.

Luke 2:6–7

How can I express the thrill of seeing our firstborn…? There are no words for the waves of joy, relief, and gratitude that surged over me. A son! In those first few days, I had sweet communion with the Lord as He taught me, through this new and profound experience, more about Himself. There were new analogies for me to understand. As I realised how deep was our love for a tiny, helpless infant who had done nothing to deserve our love at all, except to be born into our family, I had a new realisation of God's Father-love for us – entirely undeserved, but ours simply because we are His sons… Trust God to plan that a child should be the result and

8

fruit of love. And thank God He made me a woman!

Maxine Hancock (*Love, Honour and be Free*)

Dear Lord, I offer a prayer for all new-born babies today:

> *Lord, look upon this helpless child*
> *Surround him/her with protective love*
> *Enfold her/him in Your care.*

Derek R. Farrow

*   *   *

13th January

Then the Lord said: 'The outcry against Sodom and Gomorrah is so great and their sin so grievous...'

Abraham remained standing before the Lord. Then Abraham approached Him and said: 'Will you sweep away the righteous with the wicked? What if there are fifty righteous people in the city? Will you really sweep it away and not spare the place for the sake of fifty righteous people in it? Far be it from you to do such a thing – to kill the righteous with the wicked... will not the Judge of all the earth do right?'

The Lord said: 'If I find fifty righteous people in the city of Sodom, I will spare the whole place for their sake.'

Then Abraham said: 'May the Lord not be angry, but let me speak just once more. What if only ten can be found there?'

The Lord answered: 'For the sake of ten, I will not destroy it.'

Early the next morning Abraham returned to the place – he looked down towards Sodom and Gomorrah and he saw dense smoke rising from the land, like smoke from a furnace.

Genesis 18:20–25, 32–33; 19:27

*   *   *

14th January

Each of you should look not only to your own interests,
but also to the interests of others. Your attitude should be
the same as that of Jesus Christ.

Philippians 2:4

Lord, I am guilty of just considering 'me and mine' – but
when I think of all the activities and associations in this
community, it's amazing how many different interests are
covered. Thank you, Lord, for all the joy and
companionship of the organisations, choral societies,
gardening clubs, sports clubs and all the rest – even Weight
Watchers! What an opportunity for the outreach of prayer...
I will remember others today, and their needs and interests.
In my neighbourhood may Your church be seen as a caring
and interested body of people and not a 'Holy Huddle', too
heavenly minded to be of any earthly good. Bless us, Lord,
and open our eyes to see Your wonders and Your
opportunities.

*Almighty God, we thank You for the wonder of Your creation. Help us to use Your
gifts wisely, always considering the needs of others; through Jesus Christ our Lord.*
Irene Ellis

*   *   *

15th January

Then Jesus said to His disciples: 'I tell you the truth, it is
hard for a rich man to enter the kingdom of heaven... It is
easier for a camel to go through the eye of a needle than
for a rich man to enter the kingdom of God.'

Matthew 19:23

In our work we have many people whom we call Co-
Workers, and I want them to give their hands to serve people
and their hearts to love people. For, unless they come in very
close contact with them, it is very difficult for them to know
who the poor are. That's why here in Calcutta especially, we
have many non-Christians and Christians working together

at the Home for the Dying and other places. For example, an Australian came some time ago, and said he wanted to give a big donation. But after giving the donation he said: 'That is something outside of me, but I want to give something of me.' Now he comes regularly to the Home for the Dying and he shaves the men and talks to them – he wanted to give something of himself and he gives it.

Mother Teresa

Lord, I've never given until it hurts... I pray to see the opportunities within my locality where I may give my time, my effort and my care. Teach me to give the most worthwhile gift I have to offer – myself.

*   *   *

16th January

Out of the depths I cry to You, O Lord; O Lord, hear my voice.

Psalm 130:1

Today, Lord, there are so many crying out to You from the 'depths': depths of despair over unemployment, broken relationships, pain, loss of independence, fear... We take all our blessings so much for granted until, all of a sudden, life isn't going our way.

More than three hundred years ago Thomas Traherne wrote: 'Is not sight a jewel? Is not hearing a treasure? Is not speech a glory? O my Lord, pardon my ingratitude.' Forgive my down moments. Give me strength to rise above difficulties, whether they be physical, emotional or spiritual. Help me to know that I am not the first one to feel this way – but give me the assurance that to all You are a present help and source of comfort.

O God, give me strength to be victorious over myself, for nothing may chain me to this life. O raise me from these dark depths... for Thou alone understandest and canst inspire me.

(This was written by Beethoven when he realised
his deafness was incurable)

*   *   *

11

17th January

The earth is the Lord's, and everything in it, the world,
and all who live in it.

Psalm 24:1

The church has a special responsibility as the caretaker of the
earth because 'the earth is the Lord's.' I believe that if we
look at the world today, we are witnessing precisely what
Jesus was referring to when He was on His last journey to
Jerusalem. He told the disapproving Pharisees that if His
disciples were not allowed to proclaim Him then the very
stones would cry out. Today the natural world is united in
crying out to us to re-examine the way we live in the light of
our faith. It is telling us that faith is not a private matter
between us and God but something that unites us with the
whole of creation and its Creator. This is expressed in the
way we live down to the smallest details of what we buy and
how we use what we have. Jesus came, in the words of St
Paul, to bring together 'everything in the heavens and
everything on earth'.

Barbara Wood

The song grows in depth and in wideness:
The earth and its people are one.
There can be no thanks without giving
No words without deeds that are done.

Fred Kaan

* * *

18th January

As each has received a gift, employ it for one another, as
good stewards of God's varied grace.

1 Peter 4:10 (RSV)

Reading between the lines, we can see that during the birth
pangs of the early church there seem to have been

considerable rivalry regarding personal gifts. The more spectacular the gift, the greater the importance which was bestowed on that member. Of course, it all got out of hand and Paul had to send letters reprimanding the people for such insensitivity. Here in Peter's letter we note that gifts are not for personal glorification but are meant to be used for the benefit of others – we are to be stewards, chanelling whatever gifts we have been given to God's glory. This means taking a long, hard look at ourselves – praying for the humility to look around us with fresh emphasis. We need to learn how to praise and thank God for all we have, all we are and all that by His grace we may become.

Gracious God, we give thanks for all You have given. For the universe – let our wonder grow; for this world – teach us better stewardship of earth and sea and sky: let us see Your image in every human face, discern Your hand in every human culture, hear Your voice in the silence as well as the talk of neighbours.

The Uniting Church, Australia

* * *

19th January

When Jesus came into Peter's house, he saw Peter's mother-in-law lying in bed with a fever. He touched her hand and the fever left her.

Matthew 8:14

We read of many different people coming to Jesus to ask for healing, and of some who were brought by friends. Peter's mother-in-law does not appear to have been one of those. Peter didn't even ask Jesus to visit his home quickly to make the woman better. But in two brief sentences we read how Jesus saw a person in need, and with His healing touch transformed how she felt.

Lord, I know that when someone touches my hand it makes me feel comforted and lighter of heart. I pray today for those who need human touches of tenderness and Your divine touch of healing. You see, Lord, across all our hollow barriers of colour and language, You see right into our hearts and minds and You know our individual needs. You know my need. Bless me, Lord, heal me in whatever way is necessary, in the name of Jesus.

The healing of His seamless dress
Is by our beds of pain;
We touch Him in life's throng and press
And we are whole again.

John G. Whittier

*   *   *

20th January

Then Joseph said to Pharaoh: 'God has shown Pharaoh what He is about to do. Seven years of great abundance are coming throughout the land of Egypt, but seven years of famine will follow them. Then all the abundance in Egypt will be forgotten, and the famine will ravage the Land... The reason the dream was given to Pharaoh in two forms is that the matter has been firmly decided by God.

'And now let Pharaoh look for a discerning and wise man and put him in charge of the land of Egypt. Let Pharaoh appoint commissioners over the land to take a fifth of the harvest of Egypt during the seven years of abundance. They should collect all the food of these good years that are coming and store up the corn under the authority of Pharaoh, to be kept in the cities for food. This food should be held in reserve for the country, to be used during the seven years of famine that will come upon Egypt, so that the country may not be ruined by famine.'

The plan seemed good to Pharaoh and all his officials, so Pharaoh asked them, 'Can we find anyone like this man, one in whom is the spirit of God?'

Genesis 41:28–38

*   *   *

21st January

Great are the works of the Lord... He has caused His wonders to be remembered; the Lord is gracious and compassionate.

Psalm 111:2-4

Lord, I find You in so many places that I marvel at the wonder of Your ways. Help me to learn to expect this and not to be surprised. I have found You in the sacrament, in the sick and suffering, in the wildness of the hills and the sea, in the preaching of Your word, in ordinary kind people, in flowers, in trees, in small children, and often in events – in trivial events which lead me to people in need. In the sharing of their problems I may have given help, but also I have found You in them, giving me new vision, new peace, new courage. This finding of You is wonderful.

Michael Hollings and Etta Gullick

Tell out my soul, the greatness of the Lord!
Unnumbered blessings give my spirit voice:
Tender to me the promise of His word;
In God, my Saviour shall my heart rejoice!

Timothy Dudley-Smith

*   *   *

22nd January

Heal me, O Lord, and I shall be healed: save me and I shall be saved; for You are the One I praise.

Jeremiah 17:14

What do you say to a friend who is going in to hospital to have her breast removed? It is so hard to convey a word of comfort without sounding treacly or morbid or even worse, off-hand. I came across a lovely prayer for people in hospital by Joy Whyte which puts into words all that I should like said for me: 'Father of Comfort, be near those who call to You in sickness, in pain, in fear, in anxiety, in weariness and in weakness... Cover them with Your wings; keep them safe in Your care. Be near those facing difficult or uncomfortable treatment; serious surgery; prolonged hospitalisation, rehabilitation, distressing diagnosis... Thank You for those whose work brings ease – doctors, nurses, therapists, laboratory staff, radiologists, technicians, kitchen and housekeeping staff, porters, ambulance drivers and administrators... Bring quietness of mind to alarmed and worried relatives; help them to trust their loved ones to You.

> *From Thee all skill and science flow.*
> *All pity, love and care,*
> *All calm and courage, faith and hope*
> *Mingled in Your goodness there.*
>
> *Adapted from Charles Kingsley*

*　　*　　*

23rd January

> God is our refuge and strength, an ever present help in trouble.
>
> Psalm 46:1

When we hear the piercing sound of an ambulance siren, we immediately know that someone is in deep trouble. Yet the siren also tells us that help is on the way – and that's reassuring. For most of our lives people in trouble are 'other people', and so we are caught unprepared when we need help.

Lord, forgive me that usually I turn to You only in an emergency. I fail to prepare myself for times of stress, perplexity and turmoil. I come to You now to pray for Your strength, so that in that strength I may face the day.

> *O strengthen me, that, while I stand*
> *Firm on the rock and strong in Thee,*
> *I may stretch out a loving hand*
> *To wrestlers with the troubled sea.*
>
> *Frances R. Havergal*

*　　*　　*

24th January

David sang: 'The Lord is my rock, my fortress and my
deliverer; my God is my rock, in whom I take refuge.

2 Samuel 22:2

As Augustus Toplady was walking through Burrington
Coombe, a storm suddenly broke. He needed shelter, and so
he squeezed into a cleft. He saw the parallel with the human
predicament and salvation through the Cross of Jesus, and
these thoughts prompted his famous hymn. As we pass, so
inadequately prepared, through the storms of life, we look
beyond ourselves for a resource that will enable us to cope.
We recognise in Jesus the one and only Resource. We need
to shelter in the everlasting arms of love. Our faith's response
to Jesus turns into substance and evidence within our lives.

Lord, I need Your shelter today – where else can I turn?
Give me the assurance that nothing can separate me from
Your love that is in Jesus Christ.

Rock of Ages, cleft for me,
Let me hide myself in Thee.

Augustus M. Toplady

*　　*　　*

25th January

The woman said to Jesus: 'Sir, give me this water so that
I won't get thirsty and have to keep coming here to draw
water.'

John 4:15

Today, more than ever before, men and women are thirsty
for something meaningful in their lives. In the woman going
to Jacob's well with her empty water jar we see someone
encountering Jesus. Her emptiness was obvious to Jesus,
even though her lifestyle had been somewhat 'hectic'. The
beauty of that story lies in the way the woman approached

Jesus with nothing, an empty water jar and an empty life. In facing her situation Jesus helped her without condemning her. He shared with her the common need for water and took the moment to offer her Living Water. He challenged her, and her life was never the same again.

Lord, I'm feeling empty... I've lost my way a bit... Fill me with the water of life. Refresh my tired soul.

> *Let the healing streams abound,*
> *Make and keep me pure within:*
> *Thou of life the fountain art,*
> *Freely let me take of Thee:*
> *Spring Thou up within my heart,*
> *Rise to all eternity.*
>
> Charles Wesley

* * *

26th January

Here a great number of disabled people used to lie – the blind, the lame, the paralysed. One who was there had been an invalid for thirty-eight years.

John 5:3

The scene at the pool of Bethesda conjures up for us a very sorry sight. And at first glance it seems very odd for Jesus to ask the man who had been paralysed for thirty-eight years whether he wanted to get well. Yet sometimes we are all guilty of holding on to something that hinders us, of hugging a disability which we use as a convenient excuse. Was Jesus addressing such a person? Did He see someone who had grown accustomed to relying on others and had given up even wanting to stand on his own feet? Jesus knew that the man did not need to stay as he was. The man, however, needed to meet and speak with Jesus before he could be cured.

Lord, how often I just sit... The years go by and I do nothing... I haven't made any effort to meet Jesus, yet I know I need Him more than anything else in the world.

We must pass by the path of communion from the presence of the many who need us to the presence of the One whom we need.

P. C. Ainsworth

*   *   *

27th January

Now Moses was tending the flock of Jethro his father-in-law, the priest of Midian, and he led the flock to the far side of the desert and came to Horeb, the mountain of God. There the angel of the Lord appeared to him in flames of fire from within a bush. Moses saw that though the bush was on fire it did not burn up. So Moses thought, 'I will go over and see this strange sight – why the bush does not burn up.'

When the Lord saw that he had gone over to look, God called to him from within the bush, 'Moses! Moses!'

And Moses said: 'Here I am.'

'Do not come any closer,' God said. 'Take off your sandals, for the place where you are standing is holy ground.' Then He said, 'I am the God of your father, the God of Abraham, the God of Isaac and the God of Jacob.' At this, Moses hid his face, because he was afraid to look at God.

The Lord said: 'I have indeed seen the misery of my people in Egypt. I have heard them crying and am concerned about their suffering.'

Exodus 3:1–8

*   *   *

28th January

Sing to the Lord a new song, for He has done marvellous things!

Psalm 98:1

We thank You, Lord: we thank You for the bread we eat, and for the people with whom we break that bread and share.

19

We thank You for the streets and buildings, for the grass and
the trees, for the bridges and the automobiles and the
farms and the ranches,
And the lakes and the fishes.
We thank You for the telephone company, for the
typewriters,
For the adding machines, for the hay, new-mown;
For the wheat, for the barley, for the vegetables.
We thank You for each other, and we know that half across
the world
We are killing parts of ourselves.
Help us to learn, O Lord, that we are one.
We confess to You, my Lord, that we don't realise what we
are doing.
Lord, forgive us. We do not understand.

From A Modern Thanksgiving by Christopher W. Jones

Sing aloud, loud, loud...
God is good, God is truth,
God is beauty – praise Him!

Percy Dearmer

* * *

29th January

For I desire mercy, not sacrifice, and acknowledgement of
God rather than burnt offerings.

Hosea 6:6

Hudson Taylor, a renowned missionary, was once asked
about the great sacrificecs he had made during his life. His
reply was brief: 'Sacrifices? I never made a sacrifice!' What a
testimony to a life given to God. And whenever you meet
someone whose service has been directed by true love they
will always reply in the same way. I think today of parents
whose lives revolve around a child with a handicap – that is
love in action. So many of us delude ourselves by thinking we
are 'doing good', and that is all God expects. God expects
our hearts, our commitment to Him and through Him our

commitment to caring about others. The truth of this is easily proved, for to love a person changes our lives so that nothing is too much trouble. How much more will this be the case for those who love God.

Jesus said: 'Go and learn what this means: I desire mercy, not sacrifice. For I have come not to call the righteous but sinners.'

Matthew 9:13

* * *

30th January

Jesus said: 'For all who draw the sword will die by the sword.'

Matthew 26:52

On 30th January 1956, Martin Luther King was addressing a meeting when he was told that his home was being attacked. The Civil Rights leader rushed home to find that his wife and baby daughter had escaped unhurt from an explosion at the front of their house. However, his supporters were seething with a desire for revenge for the attack. Such was King's faith in Jesus Christ that he was able to say to them: 'We cannot solve this problem with retaliatory violence... Remember the words of Jesus, "He who lives by the sword will perish by the sword." Jesus still cries out across the centuries, "Love your enemies." This is what we must live by. We must meet hate with love.'

In every insult, rift and war
Where colour, scorn or wealth divide:
He suffers still, yet loves the more
And lives, though ever crucified.

Brian Wren

* * *

31st January

> John answered: 'I baptise you with water. But one more powerful than I will come... He will baptise you with the Holy Spirit and with fire.'
>
> Luke 3:16

To have contact with the Holy Spirit is to be renewed. In no way can a person remain cool and apathetic. Instead they glow with an inner warmth – we could say that they are on fire for God! At whatever level we experience love, we understand its various manifestations: it may be the warm satisfaction of holding a baby in our arms, or the fires of enthusiasm unleashed when we fall in love. To meet Divine Love, the Love which stooped to share humanity with us, is to burn away all which is wrong in our lives and to begin again. Our infant baptisms are like the baptism which John gave his followers. They symbolise repentance. But to receive baptism from Jesus Himself is to be filled with His Spirit and fire.

Lord, once is not enough – renew me today.

Give us, Lord, that holy fire to renew us day by day;
may we have that warmth in us to proclaim your love and power.

Gershon Anderson (Sierra Leone)

* * *

1st February

> When this man [royal official] heard that Jesus had arrived... he went to Him and begged Him to come and heal his son, who was close to death.
>
> John 4:47

At this very moment there are thousands of desperately worried parents. And indeed, there is nothing that rips at our hearts so much as seeing a loved one suffer, whether it is our tiny baby or our 'child' of any age. To do our best to help we are willing to go to the ends of the earth – to specialists – hospitals – to court – even to God.

Lord, my heart goes today to the sick-beds of children... to the mothers and fathers whose worlds have suddenly crumbled to nothing. My prayer is that all Your children may be made whole, and that parents may have the strength to accept that sometimes that wholeness can only be achieved by letting them go to You.

Father, You have promised to be with Your children in the midst of trouble... You are with me in all that I am suffering... I want to accept what has come into my life as something You can transform and bless. Bring good out of this evil for Your glory. In Jesus' name, Amen.

Mary Batchelor

* * *

2nd February

The Lord gives strength to His people. The Lord blesses His people with peace.

Psalm 29:11

This is my prayer to Thee, my Lord – strike at the root of penury in my heart.
Give me the strength lightly to bear my joys and sorrows.
Give me the strength to make my love fruitful in service.
Give me strength never to disown the poor.
Give me strength to raise my mind high above daily trifles.
And give me the strength to surrender my strength to Thy will with love.

Rabindranath Tagore

I kneel before the Father, from whom the whole family in heaven and on earth derives its name. I pray that out of His glorious riches He may strengthen you with power through His Spirit in your inner being, so that Christ may dwell in your hearts through faith.

Paul's prayer for the Ephesians, 3:14–17

* * *

3rd February

The Lord said: 'Make an alter of acacia wood for burning incense. It is to be square, a cubit long and a cubit wide and two cubits high – its horns of one piece with it. Overlay the top and all the sides and the horns with pure gold, and make a gold moulding around it. Make two gold rings for the altar below the mouldings – two on appropriate sides – to hold the poles used to carry it. Make the poles of acacia wood and overlay them with gold. Put the altar in front of the curtain that is before the ark of the Testimony – before the atonement cover that is over the Testimony – where I will meet with you...

'Once a year Aaron shall make atonement on its horns. This annual atonement must be made with the blood of the atoning sin offering for the generations to come. It is most holy to the Lord.'

Exodus 30: 1–7, 10

*　　*　　*

4th February

To the peoples, nations and men of every language, who live in all the world: It is my pleasure to tell you about the miraculous signs and wonders that the Most High God has performed for me!

Daniel 4:2

When my husband died a Christian friend expressed his faith in God's perfect timing. At that point I was unconvinced – I hadn't been ready! Yet when I was able to look objectively at the situation I was able to say, Yes, God's timing is perfect. I take comfort in the knowledge that God is not a God of past works and wonders but a living God who works in and through the lives of those who give themselves to Him. Because God has guided my life I can look back with gratitude – I can look forward with hope – and as I pray I look upwards with confidence. My God reigns! It is my pleasure to tell you...

24

*　　*　　*

5th February

> Then Jesus said to Thomas: 'Put your finger here; see my hands.'
>
> John 20:27

That beautiful fifteenth-century drawing of the praying hands is as familiar as pictures of the Lord's Supper or *The Light of the World*. The artist was Albrecht Durer and the hands he drew were those of his brother Franz. When the boys were young they were both keen artists, but the family was too poor to pay for both boys to train. Franz elected to work as a labourer whilst Albrecht trained. Perhaps Franz would be able to go to art school later. However, as the years passed Franz's hands became stiff through hard work, and he never went to train as an artist. So it is a touching memorial to a brother's sacrifice that Albrecht has left us. The hands which helped him are portrayed as those of someone in prayer – they are hands which have not been trained for drawing on paper, but which are instead skilled in drawing upon God.

Lord God, whose Son Jesus, my Saviour, had the firm hands of a carpenter, give to my hands the qualities of firmness, gentleness and sensitivity. May I never be discouraged by the rejection of my helping hands, since the hands of Jesus were pierced and torn for mankind.

*　　*　　*

6th February

> Moses said to the Lord, 'O Lord, I have never been eloquent, neither in the past nor since you have spoken to your servant. I am slow of speech and tongue.'
>
> Exodus 4:10

25

What a wonderful comfort it is that we do not have to attain a certain standard of eloquence before we can approach our God! In essence it is not the words from our mouths which matter, but the depth to which we feel within our inmost hearts. There are indeed times when words won't come; then our tears bear eloquent testimony to our need. There are times when words are unnecessary – a smile is our prayer of encouragement.

Lord, I come today in prayer... just plain old me... in humble gratitude for all You have done in my life and in simple trust for all that in Your mercy and love You will do in the future, for Jesus Christ's sake.

Fear not because your prayer is stammering, your words feeble and your language poor. Jesus can understand you.

J. C. Ryle

* * *

7th February

The sin of Judah is written with a pen of iron; with a point
of diamond it is engraved on the tablet of their heart...
Jeremiah 17:1 (RSV)

An uncut, unpolished diamond is indeed a drab piece of grit! It would be very easily trodden under foot without a second thought. Seeing the processes of cutting and polishing diamonds in a diamond factory gave me new insight about this precious stone. A diamond can only be cut by a diamond and is polished by diamond dust. I feel that this says something about human hearts, which are pretty drab and unexceptional until cut or broken. In that state new facets of our natures are revealed and, if we allow ourselves to be polished by the diamond dust of life's experiences, those revealed facets will shine with the light of Christ's love. There is no harder known mineral than diamond, none so enduring, none so beautiful. There is no stronger emotion than love – love endures to the uttermost, and eyes alight with love reflect the beauty of Jesus.

*   *   *

8th February

Jesus said: 'For the Son of Man came to seek and to save what was lost.'

Luke 19:10

When life has battered you – when you are feeling broken and have had the stuffing knocked right out of you – that's when you need to hang on to Jesus' words. No-one is ever beyond spiritual repair. Jesus alone knows our true value and He is willing to restore us. The King James version of the 23rd Psalm says, 'He restoreth my soul.' In fact, if you look closely at the Gospels you will find that Jesus made it clear that it was just for the needy and broken, the social and physical casualties, that He came to live and die. When we are transformed, restored and renewed in His love, our own personal worth and the whole of life takes on a new value.

We have heard a joyful sound:
Jesus saves!
Spread the gladness all around:
Jesus saves!

Priscilla Jane Owens

*   *   *

9th February

Dear friends, let us love one another, for love comes from God. Everyone who loves has been born of God and knows God.

1 John 4:7

There's a quiet understanding when we're gathered in the Spirit,
It's a promise that He gives us, when we gather in His name:
There's a love we feel in Jesus, there's a manna that He feeds us,
It's a promise that He gives us when we gather in His name.

And we know when we're together, sharing love and understanding,
That our brothers and our sisters feel the oneness that He brings.
Thank You, thank You, thank You, Jesus, for the way You love and feed us,
For the many ways You lead us, thank You, thank You, Lord.

Tedd Smith

Lord, sometimes I feel overwhelmed by the kindness and care shown to me. I don't deserve it – but Lord, it does help me so much. I thank You that these expressions of love are a sharing of Your love by people who know You. Help me to respond... draw me closer so that I may love more deeply.

*   *   *

10th February

The Lord said to Moses: 'Speak to the entire assembly of Israel and say to them. ''Be holy because I, the Lord your God, am holy.

'''Each of you must respect his mother and father, and you must observe my Sabbaths. I am the Lord your God...

'''Do not steal. Do not lie. Do not deceive one another. Do not swear falsely by my name and so profane the name of your God. I am the Lord.

'''Do not defraud your neighbour or rob him... Do not curse the deaf... Do not pervert justice; do not show partiality to the poor or favouritism to the great, but judge your neighbour fairly.

'''Do not go about spreading slander among your people... Do not seek revenge or bear a grudge against one of your people, but love your neighbour as yourself. I am the Lord. Keep my decrees.'' '

Leviticus 19:1–3, 11–19

*   *   *

11th February

Then Jesus told Thomas: 'Because you have seen me,
you have believed; blessed are those who have not seen
and yet have believed.'

John 20:29

Poor old 'doubting Thomas'! Haven't we all experienced
doubt? Martin Luther said: 'The art of doubting is easy, for
it is an ability that is born with us.' Yes, we've all done it –
either the little panicky doubt or the hurt, muddled rejection
we feel when our minds cannot cope.

Lord, You know, You understand. You are there in my
doubts as well as in my certainties. If it wasn't for You there
would be neither doubt nor certainty. Without You there
would be nothing. Lord, hold out Your hand to me as You
did for Thomas, so that I may know that my Lord and God is
within me and around me in every moment of my day.

*Dear Lord, Although I am sure of my position I am unable to sustain it without
Thee. Help me or I am lost.*

Martin Luther

*   *   *

12th February

Now this is eternal life: that they may know You, the only
true God, and Jesus Christ whom You have sent.

John 17:3

What is eternal life? It is so easy for Christians to talk in
pious phrases! The essence of eternal life is its perfect quality
rather than its endless duration. (I am not at all sure that
time means anything after death: it is purely a human
limitation.) Therefore, eternal life means the life that Christ
longs for us to have. Eternal life begins now – as soon as a
person finds Christ. It continues even more wonderfully after
death. Perhaps we can only begin to understand the true

meaning of life when we have grasped something of the meaning of death.

David Watson

> *Now is eternal life,*
> *If risen with Christ we stand,*
> *No more we fear death's ancient dread:*
> *In Christ arisen from the dead.*

George W. Briggs

*　　*　　*

13th February

But the Lord is in His holy temple; let all the earth be silent before Him.

Habakkuk 2:20

Lord, the Scripture says: 'There is a time for silence and a time for speech.' Saviour, teach me the silence of humility, the silence of wisdom, the silence of love, the silence of perfection, the silence that speaks without words, the silence of faith. Lord, teach me to silence my own heart that I may listen to the gentle movement of the Holy Spirit within me and sense the depths which are of God.

Translation of a 16th century Frankfurt Prayer

> *Lo, God is here, let us adore!*
> *How awe-inspiring is this place.*
> *Let all within us feel his power*
> *And silent bow before His face:*
> *We know His power, His grace we prove;*
> *Serve Him with fear – with reverence love.*

Gerhard Tersteegen

*　　*　　*

14th February

Jesus said: 'The second [commandment] is this: "Love your neighbour as yourself." '

Mark 12:31

When Bishop Richard Harries was visiting South Africa he was taken to a parish in the large black African township of Soweto. Everyone belonged to house groups which met three times a week for an hour's prayer and planning, to decide what acts of neighbourliness they could carry out in the next day or so.

Forgive me, Lord, that I do not bother as I should with the concerns of my neighbours. If there is some way in which I can be more caring, please show me. There may be sickness – I could cook or shop. There may be hospital visits to be made – I could drive or baby-sit. There may be hardship, loneliness or any number of problems – a touch of compassion could make all the difference. Lord, I lay my mind open to the direction of Your Holy Spirit, and I thank You for all the times when I have been so glad of neighbourly help.

We are thy stewards; thine our talents, wisdom, skill;
Our only glory that we will thy trust fulfil;
That we thy pleasure in our neighbour's good pursue
If thou but workest in us both to will and do.

G. B. Caird

* * *

15th February

The Lord will guide you always.

Isaiah 58:11

Today is the birthday of that legendary explorer, Ernest Shackleton. During one of his expeditions to the South Pole his ship was crushed by ice. With only five men in an open boat, Shackleton set out on a voyage of 800 miles to South Georgia. Then three of them had to cross the island to get help. Shackleton wrote afterwards: 'When I look back I have no doubt that Providence guided us... I know that during that long and racking march it seemed to me often that we were four, not three. I said nothing to my companions; but afterwards Worsley said to me, ''Boss, I'd a curious feeling on that march that there was another person with us.'' '

Lord, I pray today that I may be aware of Your guiding presence with me – whatever happens.

> *While life's dark maze I tread,*
> *And griefs around me spread,*
> *Be Thou my guide.*

Ray Palmer

*   *   *

16th February

For all have sinned and fall short of the glory of God, and are justified freely by His grace through the redemption that came by Jesus Christ.

Romans 3:24

These contemporary words of encouragement were found in a church magazine: 'How different life would be if every human failure could be erased without anyone knowing about it, just as mistakes can be erased on a word processor. But life is not like that! Every act and word, and even every thought, is irrevocable. But we can take heart. Through the advances in technology all our typing mistakes can be put right and all the crooked lines can be made straight – justified. That can remind us of the death and resurrection of Jesus. Through His death and our personal faith in Him, our sins, no matter how bad, have been erased, and we can be made straight – justified – freely by His grace!'

> *Believe in Him that died for thee,*
> *And, sure as He hath died,*

Thy debt is paid – thy soul is free,
And thou art justified.

Charles Wesley

*   *   *

17th February

The Lord said to Samuel: 'The Lord does not look at the things man looks at. Man looks at the outward appearance, but the Lord looks at the heart.'...

So [Samuel] asked Jesse, 'Are these all the sons you have?'

'There is still the youngest,' Jesse answered, 'but he is tending the sheep.'

Samuel said, 'Send for him.'...

So he sent and had him brought in. He was ruddy, with a fine appearance and handsome features.

Then the Lord said, 'Rise and anoint him; he is the one.'

So Samuel took the horn of oil and anointed David in the presence of his brothers, and from that day on the Spirit of the Lord came upon David in power.

1 Samuel 16:7–13

*   *   *

18th February

Jesus said: 'The kingdom of God is like a mustard seed, which is the smallest seed you plant in the ground. Yet when planted, it grows and becomes the largest of all garden plants.'

Mark 4:31

Lord, teach me to ask in faith. I pray for wars to cease, but I am half-hearted because I don't believe man could stop being greedy, so I think there will always be war. I pray that people will become more loving and tolerant to each other, but I don't really think they will change. I pray for people to recover from their illnesses, or if they don't that they will grow like You and learn from their pain, but I ask half-heartedly, not believing. Lord, save me from being cynical and give me faith as a grain of mustard seed which will grow and flourish. Jesus, I ask this in Your name.

Etta Gullick and Michael Hollings

Lord, I pray for faith – a child-like, praying love, a trusting, open faith which is not too proud to have a small beginning, and will flourish in Your love, becoming the greatest source of strength in my life.

* * *

19th February

Jesus asked: 'Who are my mother and brothers?'

Mark 3:33

The word 'church' in Kenyan ethnic languages is translated as 'community' or 'gathering'. This underlines the great sense of community in Kenya. The church is a community. Individual Christianity does not appeal very much to Kenyans. To be is to be in a community... Fellowship and caring – both joy and sorrow – is the norm of the day. Therefore turning to the living God sometimes involves the whole community, family or even village, especially in the rural areas where the sense of community is still very strong. Thus community evangelism is vital. The church replaces the traditional community. The African notion of the extended family becomes significant – the family of God throughout the whole world – transcending tribal and ethnic limitations.

John L. Shabaya (Kenya)

Lord, I pray for those whose families are out of easy reach, for young parents in new and unfamiliar surroundings, for parents, grandparents and other family members in isolation. Today may the members of Your church be to those in need a real family, giving love and support and friendship.

* * *

20th February

'I have had enough, Lord,' Elijah said. 'Take my life; I
am no better than my ancestors.'

1 Kings 19:4

I saw a poster recently that impressed me deeply. It was a
picture of a man sitting on a park bench looking depressed
and disconsolate. His arms were folded across his chest, and
there was a look of resignation in his face. The caption read,
'I give up.' When I first saw this poster, I looked at it for a
few moments and turned away, but then my eye was
attracted to something on the right-hand corner of the poster.
It was a picture of a black hill and on it a very tiny cross.
These words, barely perceptible, were printed beneath it: 'I
didn't.' Feel like giving up at this moment? Then lift your
eyes to the cross. The one who triumphed over all obstacles
holds out His hands toward you. Take His hand, and in His
strength and power – try again!

Selwyn Hughes

Take my life –
Take my hands – my voice – my will...
Take my heart – my love – myself
And I will be ever, only, all for Thee

*　　*　　*

21st February

As a father has compassion on his children, so the Lord
has compassion on those who fear Him: for He knows
how we are formed...

Psalm 103:13-14

One of the most common wails from an unhappy person is,
'Nobody understands!' It's no wonder there are
misunderstandings in life, because the way we each behave is
perverse, if not sometimes downright silly. The human
personality is desperate not to be exposed. We fear that any

exposure of our true feelings may result in rejection, and so on go the layers of self-defence.

Lord, I am guilty of hiding myself from those nearest to me and from You. I've dumped my anger onto others, I've feigned humility, I've talked too much in case someone else gets a chance of getting underneath my protection. How can people understand me? But Lord, You know my most secret feelings and fears. You know and understand and You never reject anyone. Help me to be myself and to be honest in my relationships with others. I will trust Your love to dispel misunderstandings.

Therefore each of you must put off falsehood and speak truthfully to his neighbour, for we are all members of one body... Get rid of all bitterness, rage and anger... along with every form of malice.

Ephesians 4:25,31

*   *   *

22nd February

You will seek me and find me when you seek me with all your heart.

Jeremiah 29:13

Total commitment is what the Lord is after. A flirtation, a half-and-half attitude won't do. Repeatedly it is the attitude of the heart that is called into question. If we think we have to labour night and day to seek God with a mighty concentration of human effort, we're wrong. All we need is a pure, heartfelt desire to seek Him for Himself alone, and then He lets us find Him – like a mother who plays hide-and-seek with a very small child simply to give him pleasure and deliberately allows a bit of herself to stick out of her hiding place so that the child will soon find her and experience joy in the search. It's great passages from Scripture like this (Jeremiah 29:11–14) that underline the simplicity of God's love for His children.

Delia Smith

Then, Father, grant this childlike heart
That I may come to Christ, and feel His hands on me in blessing laid,
Love-giving, strong to heal.

S. A. Brooke

*   *   *

23rd February

Be kind and compassionate to one another, forgiving each
other, just as in Christ, God forgave you.

Ephesians 4:32

The hymn written by Kate Barclay Wilkinson is full of
meaning for me. It reflects my own longing for Christ's
gentle compassion, which is so difficult for the human, selfish
nature to attain.

Lord, I lay at Your feet my self – my whole self. Take me
and fill me with Your divine compassion. Forgive me and
strengthen me for the demands of each hour. I would live as
Jesus Christ would have me live.

May the mind of Christ my Saviour live in me from day to day,
By His love and power controlling all I do or say.

May the peace of God my Father rule my life in everything,
That I may be calm to comfort sick and sorrowing.

May the love of Jesus fill me as the waters fill the sea;
Him exalting, self abasing – this is victory.

Kate Barclay Wilkinson

*   *   *

24th February

Solomon rose from before the altar of the Lord, where he
had been kneeling... He stood and blessed the whole
assembly of Israel in a loud voice, saying:
Praise be to the Lord, who has given rest to His people

Israel just as He promised. Not one word has failed of all the good promises He gave through His servant Moses. May the Lord our God be with us as He was with our fathers; may He never leave or forsake us. May He turn our hearts to Him, to walk in all His ways and to keep the commands He gave our fathers. And may these words of mind, which I have prayed before the Lord, be near to the Lord our God day and night, that He may uphold the cause of His servant and the cause of His people Israel according to each day's need, so that all the peoples of the earth may know that the Lord is God and that there is no other. But your hearts must be fully committed to the Lord our God, to live by His decrees and obey His commands.

1 Kings 8:54–61

*   *   *

25th February

Do not be overcome by evil: but overcome evil with good.

Romans 12:21

Charles Kingsley was a devout Christian who was keenly aware of the poverty and deprivation in the world. This prayer of his reflects his direct and honest approach to his own life and to his Lord: 'We let the world overcome us; we live too much in continual fear of the chances and changes of mortal life. We let things go too much their own way. We try too much to get what we can by our own selfish wits, without considering our neighbours. We follow too much the ways and fashions of the day, doing and saying and thinking anything that comes uppermost, just because there is so much around us. Free us from selfish interests and guide us, good Lord, to see Your way and to do Your will.'

Dear Lord, quieten my spirit and fix my thoughts on Your will... for in Your will alone is our peace.

George Appleton

*   *   *

38

26th February

Have mercy on me, O God, according to Your unfailing love... wash away all my iniquity and cleanse me from my sin.

Psalm 51:1-2

> *O that mine eyes might closèd be*
> *To what concerns me not to see;*
>
> *That deafness might possess mine ear*
> *To what concerns me not to hear;*
>
> *That truth my tongue might closely tie*
> *From ever speaking foolishly:*
>
> *That no vain thought might ever find*
> *A welcome in my wayward mind;*
>
> *Wash, O Lord, and purify my heart*
> *And make it clean in every part;*
>
> *That by each deed, each word, each thought*
> *Glory may to my God be brought.*
>
> *And when my heart is clean, Lord, keep it too,*
> *For that is more than I can do!*
> *Thomas Ellwood (1639–1713) – Quaker friend of Milton, Fox and Penn*

Lord, teach me today to listen. Saviour, teach me to silence my heart that I may listen to the gentle movement of the Holy Spirit.

from a 16th-century German prayer

*　　*　　*

27th February

Jesus said. 'Father, forgive them, for they do not know what they are doing.'

Luke 23:34

We all find it easy to get along with people who treat us nicely; the test comes in how we deal with people who do not. Our natural instinct is to strike back and treat them in the same way – to hurt them and get revenge against them, in other words. But that is wrong, and it never succeeds in getting the other person to respect us and be our friend. Jesus gave us another way – the way of love. Furthermore, Jesus demonstrated that in His own life, even praying for those who nailed Him to the cross.

Dr Billy Graham

> *With broken heart and contrite sigh,*
> *Forgive this sinner, Lord, I cry:*
> *Thy pardoning grace is rich and free –*
> *O God, be merciful to me.*

Cornelius Elven

*　　*　　*

28th February

Amos answered: 'I was neither a prophet nor a prophet's son... But the Lord took me from tending the flock and said to me, "Go, prophesy to my people." '

Amos 7:14

Relatively few people set out in life to dedicate their lives to the Lord. The disciples Peter, James and John were fishermen. Paul was the scourge of Jesus' followers, a strict Pharisee. Moses, David and Amos were shepherds. Many lives, both in biblical times and in every generation since, in every continent, have been redirected by 'the call of the Lord'. Wilfred Grenfell, who was born on 28th February 1867, trained to be a doctor. He had no particular interest in the Bible, but at a gospel tent meeting he suddenly felt called by Jesus. He became a doctor to the Mission to Deep Sea Fishermen, worked amongst Eskimos, and built a childrens' home and a hospital in Labrador. After hearing the call, he served his Lord and the people faithfully.

Jesus call us!...
Day by day His clear voice soundeth,
Saying, 'Christian, follow me.'

Cecil Frances Alexander

*   *   *

1st March

Praise the Lord, O my soul; all my inmost being, praise
His holy name. Praise the Lord, O my soul, and forget
not all His benefits.

Psalm 103:1-2

Millions of pounds are spent in the pursuit of youth and
beauty – on creams, potions, cosmetic surgery and beauty
therapy. But I've just read that the greatest rejuvenator of all
is free! What is it? A smile! How often do we say of a person,
'They look quite different when they smile.' They do – and
so do we.

Lord, forgive me that I bring You my moans by the
sackful. It's easy to make wingeing a habit, and criticising
others almost becomes second nature. Help me today to
praise, to forget about what other'people are doing or saying,
and to centre my soul on thanksgiving. I will give my soul a
'face-lift' and rejuvenate my heart with gladness. I am loved
and guided and saved through the life, death and
resurrection of Jesus Christ... Praise Him!

Praise to the Lord, the Almighty, the King of creation.
O my soul praise Him, for He is my health and salvation!
All you hear – brothers and sisters draw near –
Praise Him in glad adoration.

Joachim Neander

*   *   *

2nd March

Jesus said: 'For if you forgive men when they sin against you, your heavenly Father will also forgive you.'

Matthew 6:14

Jesus, through the power of the Holy Spirit, go back into my memory as I sleep. Every hurt that has ever been done to me – heal that hurt. Every hurt that I have ever caused another person – heal that hurt. All the relationships that have been damaged in my whole life that I'm not aware of – heal those relationships. But, Lord, if there is anything I need to do – if I need to go to a person because they are still suffering from my hand, bring me to awareness of that person. I ask to be forgiven. Remove whatever bitterness may be in my heart, Lord, and fill the empty spaces with Your love. Amen.

Anon

'Forgive our sins as we forgive'
You taught us, Lord to pray,
But You alone can grant the grace
To live the words we say.

Rosamond E. Herklots

*   *   *

3rd March

Then the word of the Lord Almighty came to me: 'Ask all the people of the land and the priests, ''When you fasted and mourned in the fifth and seventh months for the past seventy years, was it really for me that you fasted? And when you were eating and drinking, were you not just feasting for yourselves? Are these not the words the Lord proclaimed through the earlier prophets when Jerusalem and its surrounding towns were at rest and prosperous, and the Negev and the western foothills were settled?'' '

And the word of the Lord came again to Zechariah: 'This is what the Lord Almighty says: ''Administer true justice, show mercy and compassion to one another. Do

42

not oppress the widow or the fatherless, the alien or the poor. In your hearts do not think evil of each other.''

'But they refused to pay attention, stubbornly they turned their backs and stopped up their ears. They made their hearts as hard as flint and would not listen to the law or to the words that the Lord Almighty had sent by His Spirit through the earlier prophets.'

Zechariah 7:4–13

*　　*　　*

4th March

As Jesus and his disciples were on their way, he came to a village where a woman named Martha opened her home to him.

Luke 10:38

We respond to your invitation, O God. As we are we come. We offer to you the hostilities that shape us, the hostilities we carry, the hostilities that carry us... Move us from hostility to hospitality. Create in us a space, a room, a place – a free and friendly space where the stranger may be welcomed:
- that we may be at home in our own house,
- that we may be healed of the hurts we carry in the soul,
- that we may know brother and sisterhood,
- that we may know kindness,
- that we may laugh easily...

May we be at home with you, with our neighbour and with ourselves.

John M. Scott

Keep on loving each other as brothers. Do not forget to entertain strangers, for by so doing some people have entertained angels without knowing it.

Hebrews 13:1–2

*　　*　　*

5th March

Jesus said: 'Now that I, your Lord and Teacher, have washed your feet, you also should wash one another's feet. I have set you an example that you should do as I have done for you.'

John 13:14

No man can love God without loving his fellow-men. If he says he does, then he does not know what loving God means. That is why the social gospel is never an addendum to Christianity but always the very centre of Christianity. If you believe that God was sufficiently concerned with humanity to take humanity upon Himself then you must also believe that God is concerned that men and women should have decent conditions to live in. It is blindness to think that we can meet Christ in the Sacrament if we comfortably forget that he said that what we do and do not do to our fellow-men is done and not done to him.

Dr William Barclay

We have been calling men to services, when what they wanted was the call to service.
Studdert Kennedy

* * *

6th March

A man with leprosy came and knelt before Jesus and said, 'Lord, if you are willing you can make me clean.' Jesus reached out his hand and touched the man.

Matthew 8:2

The Scriptures remind us that Jesus broke through all the stigmas of His day and His culture. He touched, He walked with, He prayed with, He ate with and He entered the homes of those who were stigmatized. My faith tells me that just as Jesus was ever ready to identify completely with the suffering of those who were outcasts and rejected of His day, Jesus is with those today... The Jesus of the Scriptures is the self-same Jesus who would say: 'Be not afraid, be not ashamed... There is nothing, no blemish, no stigma, no reality, no form of being that separates us from God's love and God's acceptance.'

Cathie Lyons

For I am convinced that neither death nor life, neither angels nor demons, neither the present nor the future, nor any powers, neither height nor depth, nor anything else in all creation will be able to separate us from the love of God that is in Christ Jesus our Lord.

Romans 8:38–39

*   *   *

7th March

Jesus replied: 'Love the Lord your God with all your heart and with all your soul and with all your mind. This is the first and greatest commandment. And the second is like it: 'Love thy neighbour as yourself.'

Matthew 22:37–38

God – let me be aware.
Let me not stumble blindly down the ways,
Just getting somehow safely through the days,
Not even groping for another hand,
Not even wondering why it all was planned...

Stab my soul fiercely with other's pain,
Let me walk seeing horror and stain.
Let my hands, groping, find another's hand,
Give me the heart that divines, understands,
Please keep me eager just to do my share.
God – let me be aware.

Miriam Teichner

My prayer now is for all those who need the comfort and support of their neighbours – and for Your holy strength to flow through those who seek to be loving neighbours. You know the need, Lord; guide and hold us.

*   *   *

8th March

Jesus said: 'For whoever wants to save his life will lose it,
but whoever loses his life for me and the gospel will save
it.'

Mark 8:35

An eminent American psychiatrist gave this advice to his
students: 'If you come across someone who is on the verge of
a nervous breakdown, get them to go across the tracks [that
is, to go to the poor part of town] and do something positive
for them. You may not always be successful, but if you can
motivate them to help others, then the threatened nervous
breakdown will dissolve of its own accord.'

When I look back, Lord, I recognise that at my lowest
times I've been depressed because I've been so full of 'me',
unable to see beyond my own nose. Help me to understand
Your teaching that it is only in forgetting myself that I can
find the peace of Your kingdom, only in losing my life in
Your name that I can find everlasting life.

*Lord, I pray for men and women verging on nervous breakdowns. I pray for those they
live with, for the tangle of conflicting emotions which can make every word or action
misunderstood. Lord, I pray for Your calm, Your assurance and patience. The
healing will take time, but time is Your gift.*

*   *   *

9th March

Hear my voice when I call, O Lord... My heart says to
you, 'Seek His face!' Your face, Lord, I will seek.

Psalm 27:7–8

To be with God wondering... that is adoration.
To be with God gratefully... that is thanksgiving.
To be with God ashamed... that is contrition.
To be with God with others on the heart... that is intercession.
The secret is the quest of God's presence:
'Thy face, Lord, will I seek.'

Michael Ramsey

46

Thou callest me to seek Thy face – 'tis all I wish to seek;
To attend the whispers of Thy grace and hear Thee inly speak.

Charles Wesley

* * *

10th March

Jesus said: 'Be careful not to do your "acts of righteousness" before men, to be seen by them. If you do, you will have no reward from your father in heaven.

'So when you give to the needy, do not announce it with trumpets, as the hypocrites do in the synagogues and on the streets, to be honoured by men. I tell you the truth, they have received their reward in full. But when you give to the needy, do not let your left hand know what the right hand is doing, so that your giving may be in secret. Then your Father, who sees what is done in secret, will reward you...

'When you pray, go into your room, close the door and pray to your Father, who is unseen. Then your Father, who sees what is done in secret, will reward you. And when you pray, do not keep on babbling like pagans, for they think they will be heard because of their many words. Do not be like them, for your Father knows what you need before you ask Him.

Matthew 6:1–5, 7–8

* * *

11th March

When Jesus spoke again to the people He said, 'I am the light of the world. Whoever follows me will never walk in darkness, but will have the light of life.'

John 8:12

There are so many comparisons between light and love in the Gospels that at times they almost come to mean the same thing. The artist Vincent van Gogh left a beautiful verbal picture for us when he said: 'There is the same difference in a person before and after he is in love as between an unlighted lamp and one that is burning. The lamp was there and was a good lamp, but now it sheds light too, and that's its real function.'

Yes, Lord, I can see the truth in that. Help me to shine today with the light of Your love and to radiate Your warmth.

> *The light of the world was He;*
> *But men loved darkness more than light;*
> *With evil deeds of pride and hate*
> *They scorned God's love and chose the night.*
>
> *But light unconquered shone again;*
> *No cross, no tomb its power could bind:*
> *In glory, Love and Life arose*
> *To shine for ever on mankind.*

Albert F. Bayly

* * *

12th March

The son said: 'Father, I have sinned against heaven and against you. I am no longer worthy to be called your son.'

Luke 15:21

Jesus' parable of the prodigal son is sometimes called the parable of the waiting Father. In Lent we focus our thoughts on penitence. This ancient prayer from the east, which may have been known to Jesus, speaks for all souls who recognise their need of forgiveness:

All that we ought to have thought but have not thought;
All that we ought to have said and have not said;
All that we ought to have done and have not done;
All that we ought not to have thought and yet have
   thought;
All that we ought not to have spoken and yet have spoken;
   All that we ought not to have done and yet have done;
   For thought, words and works, we pray, O God,
         for forgiveness.

Lord have mercy on me.
Christ have mercy on me.
Lord have mercy on me.

*   *   *

13th March

Jesus said: 'Whoever drinks the water I give him will never thirst. Indeed, the water I give will become in him a spring of water welling up to eternal life.'

John 4:14

In March 1989, Alec Forman led a team of well-diggers during a seven-week project to dig and line three wells in the remote village of Djeba in Mali. It was very much a joint project with the village: Mission Aviation Fellowship provided the skilled well diggers, and the materials for the lining had been bought from funds raised by Christians in the USA, the UK and Australia. The villagers provided food and shelter and willing hands! As well as enabling the village to have its own water supply, the workers prayed for the Living Water to come to the village. The previous year Alec had shown the film *Jesus* to the people, which they now asked to see again. The well operation was a great success. Also, following the film outreach, eleven villagers found Jesus Christ – they will never thirst again.

> *See the streams of living waters*
> *Springing from eternal love,*
> *Well supply Thy sons and daughters*
> *And all fear of want remove.*

John Newton

*   *   *

14th March

When Herod saw Jesus, he was greatly pleased... From what he had heard about Him, he hoped to see Him

49

perform some miracle. He plied Him with many
questions, but Jesus gave him no answer.

Luke 23: 8-9

The silence of Jesus implied not the greatness of their
questions but rather the littleness of them. There are some
who decide that Jesus has nothing to tell them worth hearing,
when in reality they have asked Him nothing morally worth
answering. Their bucket has not reached the water – and yet
they go away to inform their world that the well is dry!'

This insight into our human arrogance was written in the
last century by P. C. Ainsworth, but what a ring of truth it
has for me today. Forgive me Lord, that I bombard You with
questions and then feel let down because You seem to have
no answer for me. You are God, I worship You in trust...
Your silence will be my peace... Your answers will be
revealed to me when You see that I am ready.

> Drop Thy still dews of quietness down
> Till all our strivings cease...
> Take from our souls the strain and stress
> And let our ordered lives confess
> The beauty of Thy peace.

J. G. Whittier

*   *   *

15th March

Jesus went to Nazareth, where He had been brought up,
and on the Sabbath day He went into the synagogue, as
was His custom.

Luke 4:16

> Father, I thank You for anointing Christ with the Spirit
>   to preach good news to me.
> For I am poor and have no spiritual resources
>   except for those Christ gives me.
> I am a captive to my own desires and cannot find release
>   unless Christ flings open my prison door.
> I am blind and hopelessly lost unless Christ who is the
>   Light of the World comes and shows me the Way.

50

My imagination takes me into the shadows of that synagogue in Nazareth... the good news comes to me with a fresh sound. Can it really be meant for me, this Light and Love and Eternity? I beg to know it is for me, I need it so much... I wait, I pray, I feel... I close my eyes.

*   *   *

16th March

Then Jesus told him: 'Because you have seen me, you have believed: blessed are those who have not seen me and yet have believed.'

John 20:29

There is only one way in which, with the world as it is, God can show himself good in respect of man's suffering; and that is by not asking of us anything that he is not prepared to endure Himself. He must share the dirt and the sweat, the bafflement and loneliness, the pain, the weakness, yes, and the death too. That would be a God one could respect, a God who put aside all magic weapons, and did it all as one of us. A God who, when we cry out in our misery (as we all do), 'Why should this happen to me?' can answer truthfully, 'It happened to me too.' Then and then alone will our doubts be stilled, not because we understand, but because we can trust.

John Austin Baker

I am not skilled to understand what God has willed, what God has planned;
I only know at His right hand stands One who is my Saviour.
I take God at His word and deed, Christ died to save me, this I read;
And in my heart I find a need of Him to be my Saviour.

Dora Greenwell

*   *   *

51

17th March

Jesus said: 'Do not store up for yourselves treasures on earth, where moth and rust destroy, and where thieves break in and steal. But store up for yourselves treasures in heaven, where moth and rust do not destroy, and where thieves do not break in and steal. For where your treasure is, there your heart will be also.

The eye is the lamp of the body. If your eyes are good your whole body will be full of light. But if your eyes are bad, your whole body will be full of darkness. If then the light within you is darkness, how great is that darkness!

No-one can serve two masters. Either he will hate the one and love the other, or he will be devoted to the one and despise the other. You cannot serve both God and Money.'

Matthew 6:19-25

*　　*　　*

18th March

When Jesus came near the place where the road goes down to the Mount of Olives, the whole crowd of disciples began joyfully to praise God in loud voices.

Luke 19:37

There really is something very therapeutic in the sound of joyful praise. Whether it is the Salvation Army, or a toe-tapping, swaying black gospel group or a church congregation in full-throated hymn singing, the response of our hearts to God's praise uplifts us. The writer C. S. Lewis said it so vividly: 'Praise is inner health made audible.' The crowds who followed Jesus down to the Mount of Olives could not contain themselves – they were full of all they had seen and heard, and their joy and enthusiasm spilled over into spontaneous praise.

Lord, I come to You now, needing inner health and strength... I come asking for that ability to praise Your Holy Name in every part of my life.

Praise my soul the King of Heaven;
To His feet thy tribute bring.
Ransomed, healed, restored, forgiven,
Who like thee His praise should sing?
Praise Him! Praise Him!
Praise the everlasting King!

Henry F. Lyte

*　　*　　*

19th March

As they led Him away, they seized Simon from Cyrene,
who was on his way in from the country, and put the cross
on him and made him carry it behind Jesus.

Luke 23:26

I prepared to walk the Via Dolorosa, the Way of the Cross,
filled with my personal sorrow and burden of emptiness.
Walking with me was Jack, and as he shared how his
daughter had died at the age of thirty-one, leaving an eleven
day-old baby, my own heartbreak receded. We walked
together the Way of tears and agony, and the Saviour who
walked that Way two thousand years before was with us and
within us as we walked. And suddenly it didn't matter where
we were, for as Jack went on to share how his daughter's
death had brought so many to believe in Jesus, we silently
realised that the cost of God's love is the bearing of a billion
agonies, the sharing in the tears of the world. We were not
aware of time as we followed those narrow streets in old
Jerusalem – just aware of the Living Love which shines Hope
into our broken hearts.

Shun not suffering, shame or loss;
Learn of Him to bear the cross.
Turn not from His griefs away,
Learn of Jesus Christ to pray.
Christ is risen,
Saviour, teach us so to rise.

James Montgomery

*　　*　　*

20th March

You are not your own; you were bought at a price.
Therefore, honour God with your body.

1 Corinthians 6:20

If you heard that your life had been valued –
That a price had been paid on the nail;
Would you ask 'what was traded?'
*   'how much?' and 'who paid it?'*
'Who was he and what was his name?'
If you heard that His name was Jesus
Would you say that the price was doo dear?
Held to the cross, not by nails, but by love;
It was you broke His heart, not the spear.
Would you say it was worth what it cost Him?'
You say, 'No!' but the price stays the same...
He paid what He thought you were worth!
How much do you think you are worth?
What are you willing to give Him
*   in return for the price that He paid?*

Adrian Snell

Lord, I am not worthy; yet, how can I refuse to come to You
– You who gave Your very flesh and blood to pay the price of
my ransom. Lord of my life, I come.

*   *   *

21st March

Jesus said: 'It is not the healthy who need a doctor, but
the sick. I have not come to call the righteous but sinners
to repentance.'

Luke 5:31

In any illness there are certain steps which must be gone
through before a cure is possible... A man is not only a body;
a man is also a soul, a spirit and a mind. The spirit and the
mind must be right before the body can be cured. For a
complete cure two things are necessary: the best medical

treatment, willingly accepted, and the most intense prayer, faithfully offered. When that happens, the spirit is in a condition for the body to be cured. For then the grace of God co-ordinates with the skill of man, that skill which God Himself has given.

Dr William Barclay

> *There's still so much sickness and suffering today;*
> *Heal us, heal us today!*
> *We gather together for healing, and pray:*
> *Heal us, Lord Jesus!*

Peter Smith

*   *   *

22nd March

Jesus said: 'When you pray, do not keep on babbling... for your Father knows what you need before you ask Him.'

Matthew 6:7

Prayer seems to be as ancient an activity as any recorded, but what exactly is prayer? One dictionary gives this definition: 'a turning of one's soul in reverence, infinite desire and endeavour to what is highest and best'. Well, Jesus obviously noticed that many used prayer in order to show off or to attempt to influence God by the length of their prayers, and He specifically warned His followers against doing the same. The old tendencies linger still. Our subconscious attitudes are not far from those of the little boy who, according to Dr Anthony Campolo, announced: 'I'm going to bed and I'm going to be praying. Anybody want anything?' Lord, keep me simple!

> *O Thou by whom we come to God,*
> *The Life, the Truth, the Way,*
> *The path of prayer Thyself hast trod:*
> *Lord, teach us how to pray!*

James Montgomery

*   *   *

23rd March

> Then Jesus went with His disciples to a place called Gethsemane, and He said, 'Sit here while I go over there and pray.'
>
> Matthew 26:36

The Garden of Gethsemane today is a tiny oasis of quiet and other-worldliness in a sad and tension-torn city. To stand and look at the gnarled, old, stumpy olive trees, to listen to the birds and gaze at the sky, is to enter into sights and sounds that have not changed in two thousand years. In the Garden of Gethsemane I became aware of a tangible gentleness which was not merely around me, but within me as well. There was a peace which entered my life, and I knew there and then that it would never leave me. Jesus promised His peace, and sometimes we find it in unexpected places. Wherever we find it, we shall never be quite the same again. Thank You, Lord, for the peace which passes all understanding. May it rest in all our hearts today.

> *Go to dark Gethsemane,*
> *Your Redeemer's conflict see:*
> *Turn not from His griefs away,*
> *Learn of Jesus Christ to pray.*
>
> *James Montgomery*

*   *   *

24th March

> Once when Jesus was praying in private and His disciples were with Him, He asked them, 'Who do the crowds say I am?'
>
> They replied, 'Some say John the Baptist; others say Elijah; and still others, that one of the prophets of long ago has come back to life.'
>
> 'But what about you?' He asked. 'Who do you say I am?'
>
> Peter answered, 'The Christ of God.'

Jesus strictly warned them not to tell this to anyone. And He said, 'The Son of Man must suffer many things and be rejected by the elders, chief priests and teachers of the law, and He must be killed and on the third day be raised to life.'

Then He said to them all: 'If anyone would come after me, he must deny himself and take up his cross daily and follow me. For whoever wants to save his life will lose it, but whoever loses his life for me will save it. What good is it for a man to gain the whole world, and yet lose or forfeit his very self?'

Luke 9:18–25

*   *   *

25th March

He was despised and rejected by men, a man of sorrows and familiar with suffering.

Isaiah 53:3

At times we feel so crushed by events that we forget that others also have to endure such stress. It is a comfort to realise that we are part of the family of mankind, and that each one of us experiences sorrow and suffering to varying degrees. Christ suffered to the ultimate degree – we share with Him and He with us. John Woolman was an American Quaker who devoted his life to witnessing against the brutality and evil of slavery. Here is his testimony: 'I felt the depth and extent of the misery of my fellow creatures and it was heavier than I could bear... In the depths of misery O Lord, I remembered that Thou art omnipotent, that I called Thee Father... I saw that meekness under suffering was shown to us in the most affecting example of Thy Son and that Thou taughtest me to follow Him.

Lord, I pray for those who are despised and who suffer because of their colour and race; I pray for those who suffer brutality of any sort; I pray for the suffering of innocents caught up in wars and man's hatred; I pray for the starving, for those who suffer beyond all imagination. Lord, to follow

Jesus is indeed to share suffering – in that sharing be my strength.

*   *   *

26th March

The angels said to them: 'Flee for your lives! Don't look back, and don't stop anywhere in the plain!'... But Lot's wife looked back and she became a pillar of salt.

Genesis 19:17, 26

The calamity which befell Lot's wife has become truly legendary. The background to the story was that terrible things were going to happen to the evil cities of Sodom and Gomorrah. However we interpret this story from the Old Testament, there is a contemporary parable to be found in it. There is a great deal of evil in the world today, and people are often curious and intrigued and want to see it – take for instance violent videos and pornographic books and magazines. People seem drawn to go and look at disasters too – tragic news is more compelling than happy news. In being spectators we do no good, and often harrowing memories do us a great deal of emotional harm. In an emergency the spectators are nothing but a nuisance. Sadly, there are people in the church who are merely spectators, looking on from a distance... They are as alive to Christ's love as a pillar of salt.

Lord, keep me from looking back... Help me to resist being drawn towards anything which keeps me from looking to Jesus.

*   *   *

27th March

Jesus said: 'See how the lilies of the field grow. They do not labour or spin. Yet I tell you that not even Solomon in all his splendour was dressed like one of these.'

Matthew 6:28

To bring the disciples face to face with the reality of God's love and care, Jesus picked a flower. And how wonderfully aware of the Almighty Creator we can be when we are away from our concrete shells. Richard Jefferies wrote about how he came close to God in prayer out of doors... 'I was utterly alone with the sun and the earth. Lying down on the grass, I spoke in my soul... The air touched me and gave me something of itself. I saw the sea, green at the rim of the earth and blue in deeper ocean... The rich blue of the unattainable flower of the sky drew my soul towards it... By all these I prayed. Then I prayed by the sweet thyme whose little flowers I touched with my hand; by the slender grass; by the crumble of dry chalky earth I took up and let fall through my fingers... breathing the earth-encircling air, holding out my hand for the sunbeams... In deep reverence, thus I prayed.'

> For the beauty of each hour
> Of the day and of the night;
> Hill and vale and tree and flower,
> Sun and moon and stars of light:
> Gracious God to Thee we raise this our sacrifice of praise.
>
> F. S. Pierpoint

*   *   *

28th March

And Jesus took bread, gave thanks and broke it, and gave it to them, saying, 'This is my body given for you...'
Luke 22:19

Putting the Gospel and the people together, we begin a process of building a new world... Basically, peace is sharing – sharing tears, sadness, bread and sharing God – thereby creating a different form of society. Unless we realise this kind of society, we may not have war, but we will have discrimination and there will be a gap between rich and poor. This is fundamentally what Jesus did at the Last Supper. He shared His body and blood, He shared Himself. In that shared blood you can see God's kingdom being built.

I come with Christians far and near
To find, as all are fed,
The new community of love
In Christ's communion bread.

Brian A. Wren

* * *

29th March

When they came to the place called The Skull, there they crucified Him.

Luke 23:33

Jesus, the crucified pleads for me
While He is nailed to the shameful tree,
Scorned and forsaken, derided and curst
See how His enemies do their worst!
Yet, in the midst of the torture and shame,
Jesus, the crucified, breathes my name...
Wonders of wonders, Oh! how can it be?
Jesus the crucified pleads for me.

Jesus is dying in agony sore,
Jesus is suffering more and more,
Jesus is bowed with the weight of His woe
Jesus is faint with each bitter throe.
Jesus is bearing it all in my stead –
Pity Incarnate for me has bled:
Wonders of wonders it ever must be
Jesus the crucified pleads for me!

J. Sparrow-Simpson

He was despised and rejected by men, a man of sorrows, and familiar with suffering... Surely, he took up our infirmities and carried our sorrows, yet we considered him stricken by God, smitten by Him and afflicted. But He was pierced for our transgressions...

Isaiah 53:3–5

* * *

30th March

God said [to Moses]: 'Take off your sandals, for the place
where you are standing is holy ground.'

Exodus 3:5

The root of our problem is that there has been a collapse of
belief in values that have an ultimate source beyond
ourselves. Nothing is sacred, because we are the captains of
our souls and the masters of our fate. There is no holy
ground on which we fear to stand. And yet... there remains a
deep spiritual yearning for what we have lost, a yearning
which can still reverberate to the message of Easter. It is still
those who sacrifice themselves for others whom we really
admire. We have never really lost the knowledge that unless
we can allow our own greed and selfishness to die, we can
never be truly alive or free. The words, 'Christ is Risen',
that will ring tomorrow in the hearts of Christians, are words
that carry the power to transform, even now, our lost and de-
natured civilisation.

Daily Telegraph editorial

Lord, where has my sense of wonder gone? Where is my
whispered reverence for Your holy presence?... I confess the
sin of self-sufficiency, the emptiness of trusting my own
strength. Lord, my Lord and my God, breathe into my life
Your transforming, sacrificial holiness.

*   *   *

31st March

Early on the first day of the week, while it was still dark,
Mary of Magdala went to the tomb and saw that the stone
had been removed from the entrance. So she came
running to Simon Peter and the other disciple, the one
Jesus loved, and said, 'They have taken the Lord out of
the tomb, and we don't know where they have put Him.'
So Peter and the other disciple started for the tomb.

61

Both were running, but the other disciple outran Peter and reached the tomb first. He bent over and looked in at the strips of linen lying there but did not go in. Then Simon Peter, who was behind him, arrived and went into the tomb. He saw the strips of linen lying there, as well as the burial cloth that had been around Jesus' head. The cloth was folded up by itself, separate from the linen. Finally, the other disciple, who had reached the tomb first, also went inside. He saw and believed.

John 20:1–9

Lo! Jesus meets us – risen from the tomb!

*　　*　　*

1st April

As they approached the village... Jesus acted as if He were going further. But they urged Him strongly, 'Stay with us, for it is nearly evening...'

Luke 24:29

Lord of the night, thank You for the rest that each sunset brings, for the peace and quietness of late hours... for the stillness of the stars and the night. And may those who cannot sleep know the comfort of Your presence. Lord, help me to enjoy the gift of evening, let me not relive the tensions of the day that has gone; let me savour this space. Let me be refreshed. Let me rest mind and body. Let me place my trust in You, who have led me to this time and place, in You, the giver of life and light and sleep.

Frank Topping

The night has come wherein at last we rest;
God order this and all things for the best.

Petrus Herbert, d. 1571

*　　*　　*

2nd April

They found the stone rolled away from the tomb, but
when they entered they did not find the body of the Lord
Jesus.

Luke 24:2

I once heard expressed the beautiful thought that the stone
was rolled away not so that Jesus could come out of the tomb,
but so that believers might go in and see for themselves that it
is empty. He is risen! There is no grave to which we go and
mourn his death. Jesus is not restricted to the past or to the
confines of our understanding. He has burst through the
mysterious barrier between life and death. He lives to lead us
into that new existence beyond the grave. Lord, help me to
feel Your living presence; may it be my hope, my joy and my
assurance.

*While they were wondering about this, suddenly two men in clothes that gleamed like
lightning stood beside them. In their fright the women bowed down with their faces to
the ground, but the men said to them: 'Why do you look for the living among the dead?
He is not here. He is risen!'*

Luke 24:4–7

* * *

3rd April

Consider what a great forest is set on fire by a small
spark.

James 3:5

*It only takes a spark to get a fire going
And soon all those around can warm up in its glowing;
That's how it is with God's love,
Once you've experienced it
You spread His love to everyone... you want to pass it on.*

*What a wondrous time is spring when all the trees are budding,
The birds begin to sing, the flowers start their blooming;
That's how it is with God's love,*

63

Once you've experienced it
You want to sing! It's fresh as spring... you want to pass it on.

I want the world to know the Lord of Love has come to me,
I want to pass it on!

Kurt Kaiser

Lord, kindle that spark of sacred love in my heart today. I praise and worship You – and just that small spark will make all the difference to my day and to my life, for it will grow and I will pass it on.

*   *   *

4th April

As they talked and discussed these things with each other,
Jesus himself came up and walked along with them.

Luke 24:15

The two who walked along the Emmaus road had hearts heavy with confusion. They couldn't stop talking about all the things which had happened, and when they were joined by the stranger they still kept on talking. What a wonderful example Jesus gave by not crashing in on their conversation and declaring His Lordship and His Risen Presence. No, He walked quietly alongside them and let them express their hopes and fears. Jesus was the Divine Listener before He became their Divine Guide through the prophecies concerning the Messiah.

Lord, may I learn to be a good listener. People can't easily 'pull themselves together'. There are times when I myself find that I cannot snap out of how I feel. Then I long for a good listener, someone who will walk alongside me without judging or criticising, who will just be there and gently guide me through.

Talk with us, touch us tenderly,
Lead us to peace, to rest, to light.

*Dispel our darkness with Thy face
Radiant with resurrection grace.*

James A. Noble

*   *   *

5th April

Listen to your father, who gave you life, and do not despise your mother when she is old... May your mother and father be glad.

Proverbs 23:22, 25

The compilers of the Jewish Wisdom literature spoke from experience! No child seems to want to listen. I was a child once – Lord, forgive my arrogance that I find it so hard to listen even now. An old country saying about children goes: When they are young they make the arms ache and when they grow up they make the heart ache. My prayer today is for an ever-deepening sense of family loyalty, fun and togetherness. Lord, break down the barriers of misunderstanding, give joy through a surprise phone-call, don't ever let me fall into complacency over my family. Bless the spontaneous pride of mothers and fathers in their children, and may love in families reflect the love of Your world-wide family, for Jesus" sake.

I think the family is all-important... You know, your mother and your father are the two best things in your life. It's only perhaps when you lose them, in later life, that you realise that when you were young you didn't appreciate them enough.

Henry Cooper (Boxer)

*   *   *

6th April

No, in all these things we are more than conquerors through Him who loved us.

Romans 8:37

A story is told of how a father came across his young son wrestling with a huge piece of stone which was far too heavy for him to lift. The boy was red in the face with pushing and heaving. 'Are you using all your strength?' asked the father. 'Of course I am!' came the indignant reply. 'No, you're not,' said Dad. 'You haven't asked me to help yet, and I'm part of your strength.'

How easy it is to be like the boy and to forget that we have Another from whom we can draw strength. Lord, forgive me – forgive my pride, my unbelief, my arrogance, my spiritual blindness. You have offered Your strength to enable me to be more than a conqueror in life's 'heavy' days.

> *Jesus, my strength, my hope,*
> *On Thee I cast my care,*
> *With humble confidence look up*
> *And know Thou hear'st my prayer.*
> *Give me on Thee to wait till I can all things do:*
> *On Thee, Almighty to create – Almighty to renew.*
>
> Charles Wesley

*   *   *

7th April

> *I will praise You, O Lord, with all my heart:*
> *I will tell of all your wonders.*
> *I will be glad and rejoice in You;*
> *I will sing praise to Your name, O most High...*
> *The Lord reigns for ever...*
> *He will judge the world in righteousness;*
> *He will govern the peoples with justice.*
> *The Lord is a refuge for the oppressed,*
> *A stronghold in times of trouble.*
> *Those who know Your name will trust in You,*
> *For You, Lord, have never forsaken those who seek You.*
> *Sing praises to the Lord, enthroned in Zion;*
> *Proclaim among the nations what He has done...*
> *Arise, O Lord, let man not triumph;*

Let the nations be judged in Your presence...
Let the nations know they are but men.

Psalm 9:1, 2, 7-11, 19,20

*　　*　　*

8th April

'I know that my redeemer lives, and that in the end he
will stand upon the earth... I myself will see him.'

Job 19:25, 27

The Book of Job is the archetypal story about human agony,
suffering and disaster. If anything, all the tossing and
churning we do in our attempts to rationalise the meaning of
pain and suffering can make us feel worse and more hopeless.
Job was no fool, yet his unfaltering and conscious decision
was to trust God. He quietly and firmly held on to his faith.
He didn't understand – nobody ever will – he just accepted
that God, his redeemer, was alive and working in every
situation which he encountered.

Lord, when I'm baffled, when I'm distraught and even
desperate, help me to hold on to my faith... to hold on to
You.

I do not need to believe, I know.

Jung

*　　*　　*

9th April

And I heard a loud voice from the throne saying, 'Now
the dwelling of God is with men, and He will live with
them. They will be His people, and God Himself will be
with them and be their God.'

Revelation 21:3

On 9th April, 1945, the German theologian Dietrich
Bonhoeffer was taken from his cell in Flossenburg

concentration camp and executed. The prison doctor watched him as he said his last prayers. Later the doctor remarked, 'I have hardly ever seen a man die so entirely submissive to the will of God.' For Bonhoeffer death was the beginning of something else, the beginning of life without the hell of man's hatred.

Today there are many who suffer for their faith. Lord, I pray for them and for their families who wait and love so helplessly. I earnestly pray for Your kingdom of justice and peace to sweep this world.

I am so sure of God's hand and guidance that I hope I shall always be held in this certainty. You must never doubt I travel with gratitude and cheerfulness along the road where I'm being led.

Dietrich Bonhoeffer

* * *

10th April

Then will the eyes of the blind be opened and the ears of the deaf unstopped... and the tongue of the dumb shout for joy.

Isaiah 35:5–6

Lord, open our ears...
To hear what You are saying to us
in the things that happen and in the people we meet.

Open our hands...
To reach out to one another in friendship
and to help when help is needed.

Open our lips...
To share our stories with one another
and to bring comfort, inspiration, joy and laughter to each other.

Open our minds...
To discover new truth about You, about ourselves,
about each other and about our world.

Open our hearts...
To welcome one another freely –
just as You welcome us through Jesus Christ.

Based on a Corrymeela prayer

A man who had been cured of blindness by Jesus told his neighbours, 'The man they call Jesus made some mud and put it on my eyes. He told me to go to Siloam and wash. So I went and washed, and then I could see' (John 9:11). Lord, help me to do what You tell me, and then I will see with new vision.

*   *   *

11th April

I answered the king: 'If it pleases the king... let him send me to the city in Judah where my fathers are buried, so that I can rebuild it.'

Nehemiah 2:5

There are few things which are more depressing to look at than the piles of rubble on a building site. Water lies around in puddles... mud gets everywhere... things have an abandoned and forlorn air. Yet all that rubble and mess is eventually transformed into a building designed by the architect to provide comfort and security. How different the finished product is from the building site! Nehemiah's dream was to re-establish the fortress of Zion, to rebuild the walls around the holy city of Jerusalem which had been attacked and laid bare. This episode teaches us that even things which seem secure and strong are not invincible. The heart which puts its trust in stones and walls, in buildings and possessions, will be disillusioned. There is always the need to rebuild broken relationships, lives which have disintegrated, bodies and minds which need repair... Lord, make me a willing rebuilder with the bricks of love.

Build Your church, Lord,
Make it strong, Lord
Make us one, Lord, in Your power.

D. Richards

*   *   *

12th April

Simon Peter answered: 'Master, we've worked hard all
night and haven't caught anything. But, because You say
so, I will let down the nets.'

Luke 5.5

Here Jesus requested something that went completely
against a fisherman's common sense. But for Peter it was not
his knowledge, experience or skill that counted, but rather
what Jesus said. Peter did not understand, but he obeyed and
so the miracle happened. The same principle applies to us
today. Jesus may be calling us to do something which might
not seem logical to us, but if we make Peter's reply our own,
we will experience miracles. We should say, 'At your word,
Jesus, I dare to do it and I commit myself to being obedient
to Your will, your call and commission.'

*The deeds and miracles of Jesus are not actions of the past. Jesus is waiting for those
who are still prepared to take risks at His word, because they trust His power utterly.*
Text of a plaque on the wall of the church
facing the Sea of Galilee

*   *   *

13th April

He makes me lie down in green pastures, he leads me
beside quiet waters, He restores my soul.

Psalm 23:2

Lord, You know how much I need the still waters for today...
the quiet confidence amid the turmoil that is life. But

sometimes it is difficult to find the stillness. I find that even when my body is still, my mind continues to race, thinking about people, about things to do... It is hard to relax. Spinoza believed that 'All is in God, all lives and moves in God.' Yes, I believe that too, and just now I need to rest in God. There is a soothing Japanese translation of the twenty-third Psalm which goes: 'He provides me with images of stillness which restore my serenity. He anoints me with the oil of tranquility.' Lord, I believe You will do this for me...

> Beside still waters He leadeth me,
> His love will guard me tenderly.
> My grief shall pass, my doubt shall flee,
> Beside still waters He leadeth me.

> *Bernard Hamblen*

*   *   *

14th April

> There are six things the Lord hates,
> seven that are detestable to him:
> haughty eyes, a lying tongue,
> hands that shed innocent blood,
> a heart that devises wicked schemes,
> feet that are quick to rush into evil,
> a false witness who pours out lies
> and a man who stirs up dissension among brothers.

> My son, keep your father's commands
> and do not forsake your mother's teaching.
> Bind them upon your heart for ever;
> fasten them around your neck.
> When you walk, they will guide you;
> when you sleep, they will watch over you...
> For these commands are a lamp
> this teaching is a light,
> and the corrections of discipline are the way of life.

> *Proverbs 6:20–25*

*   *   *

15th April

Jesus said: 'You judge by human standards; I pass judgement on no one.'

John 8:15

> *I'm not here to judge you;*
> > *I'm here to listen to what you need to say.*
> *I'm not here to blame you;*
> > *I'm here to know how you feel.*
> *I'm not here to say,*
> > *'It shouldn't have been this way';*
> *I'm here to simply be with you*
> > *when things are not as you'd wish they were.*
> *I am your friend – and I care.*

Sudha Khristmukti

Lord God, lead us now to see in Jesus all the grace of Your holy word, lead us to know His steadfast love and tender care for all people, everywhere.

Ruth Carter

*   *   *

16th April

Philip found Nathaniel and told him: 'We have found the one Moses wrote about in the Law... Jesus of Nazareth.' 'Nazareth! Can any good thing come from there?' Nathaniel asked. 'Come and see,' said Philip.

John 1:46

Howard Booth mentions in his book *Healing through Caring* that some preachers have a card in front of them in their pulpits saying, 'We would see Jesus.' That is a salutary reminder that God works the continuing miracle of opening hearts to the daily relevance of Jesus Christ. Jesus is alive! He inspires and stimulates us today by His example of care, by His conversations and vivid stories. We 'see' Jesus through the centuries; we see how He accepted and loved people as they were. He never applied any unhealthy pressure. He was moved with compassion and lifted people forward into a new experience of life. Today we 'see' the indwelling of Jesus in lives which show His compassion for the ones in our society who feel rejected or inadequate. Lord, I have found You, I worship You... but what a lot I have to learn if I am to say to others by my life, 'Come and see for yourself!'

My prayers are for those who have no Lord to turn to: those who have deep problems... who are empty and alone... Lord God, send someone to show them Jesus.

*   *   *

17th April

'See, I have placed before you an open door that no-one can shut.'

Revelation 3:8

I know some people to whom I can go at any time – there is always a welcome, always an open door. This should be one of the hall-marks of the Christian attitude. We should be always available, always ready to listen, always wanting to care. In John's Gospel Jesus likened Himself to the door of the sheep-fold. For me, Jesus being a door means that His cross opens up the way to this new attitude to living, to His life of gentleness, understanding and love. Or to put it another way, Jesus is the doorway to the Kingdom of Heaven. That door is open to everyone who admits their need of cleansing in the precious blood. There is no charge to go in. Jesus is the door to full and free salvation.

> *Step over the threshold – don't stand at the door –*
> *Just come as you are... don't stand at the door:*
> *Your God is waiting for you.*

*   *   *

73

18th April

Every day they continued to meet together in the temple courts... They broke bread in their homes and ate together with glad and sincere hearts, praising God... and the Lord added to their number daily.

Acts 2:46

Lord, I'm in danger of turning into an awful moaning minnie. Today I will give You nothing but praise – real, sincere and heart-felt praise for Your goodness to me. Thank You for my sight and my hearing, for the way my body co-ordinates so that I can walk around without conscious effort. Thank You for the blessings of health and home and loved ones. Lord, I praise You for the new life which the Spring brings, and also for the new human lives that enter this world every second. When I think of all the wonderful miracles of life around me, I feel my praise is so small; and yet I know You will take my praise and join it with the joy of all the believers on earth and of the great company in Your keeping...

As o'er each continent and island
The dawn leads on another day,
The voice of prayer is never silent
Nor dies the strain of praise away.

John Ellerton

*   *   *

19th April

...At the name of Jesus every knee should bow, in heaven and on earth and under the earth, and every tongue confess that Jesus Christ is Lord...

Philippians 2:10

Jesus is Lord! Creation's voice proclaims it,
For by His power each tree and flower
Was planned and made.

74

Jesus is Lord! The universe declares it,
Sun, moon and stars in heaven
Cry, 'Jesus is Lord!'

Jesus is Lord! Jesus is Lord!
Praise Him with Hallelujahs
For Jesus is Lord!

Jesus is Lord! o'er sin the mighty conqueror,
From death He rose, and all His foes
Shall own His name.
Jesus is Lord! God sent His Holy Spirit
To show by works of power
That Jesus is Lord!

David J. Mansell

May the grace of the Lord Jesus Christ, and the love of God
and the fellowship of the Holy Spirit be with you all.

2 Corinthians 13:14

*   *   *

20th April

And Jesus left them and went out of the city to Bethany,
where He spent the night.

Matthew 21:17

I expect Mary, Martha and Lazarus looked forward to
receiving Jesus into their home as much as He enjoyed being
in their company. He was doubtless glad to be with a family,
since at times he must have missed his family home in
Nazareth as He toured the countryside. There is a
challenging text on display in Bethany which reads: 'Today,
as in the past, the love of Jesus seeks a refuge where He is
lovingly expected and where He can rest. He finds our hearts
are filled with distractions – people, work, our own interests.
He longs for us to empty our hearts and lovingly receive
Him.' Lord, help me to put everything aside in order to hear
Your words and to grow in Your love, so that my heart may
be a Bethany for you, and my home a Bethany for others.

O welcome is my Saviour here,
A constant guest is He.
The love in this small home we share
Sweet echoes of Bethany.

E. Rundle

*   *   *

21st April

Whoever loves money never has money enough;
whoever loves wealth is never satisfied with his income.
This too is meaningless.
As goods increase, so do those who consume them.
And what benefit are they to the owner
except to feast his eyes on them?
The sleep of a labourer is sweet,
whether he eats little or much,
but the abundance of a rich man
permits him no sleep.

I have seen a grievous evil under the sun:
wealth hoarded to the harm of its owner,
or wealth lost through some misfortune...
Naked a man comes from his mother's womb,
and as he comes, so he departs...

Moreover, when God gives any man wealth and possessions, and enables him to enjoy them, to accept his lot and be happy in his work – this is a gift of God.

Ecclesiastes 5:10–15, 19

*   *   *

22nd April

Jesus took her by the hand and said: 'My child, get up!'
Her spirit returned and at once she stood up.

Luke 8:54

I have never forgotten the words of a chaplain at a psychiatric hospital as he emphasised the importance of holding a patient's hand. Most adults feel diffident about touch – yet it can be the one point of contact someone is longing for. We all need the healing touch of encouragement; when our spirits are low a loving hand can make all the difference. The hand of Jesus will bring us alive again.

Lord, perhaps I'm thinking of myself too much. Oh give me grace to be Your kindness and gentleness to others, to offer them the hand of comfort, the hand of friendship, the hand of service, for Jesus' sake.

> *When I feel the touch*
> *Of your hand upon my life*
> *It causes me to sing a song*
> *That I love You, Lord.*
> *So from deep within,*
> *My spirit singeth unto Thee*
> *You are my King*
> *You are my God*
> *And I love You, Lord*
>
> *Keri Jones & Dave Matthews*

*   *   *

23rd April

Jesus said: 'I will ask the Father, and He will give you another Counsellor to be with you for ever – the Spirit of Truth.'

John 14:15

Jesus promised another 'Counsellor', another 'Helper' – not a something but a someone, a person like Himself. Everything Jesus was to His disciples, the Spirit can be to us, today. The Spirit can be everywhere at once, and he can also live within us, wherever we are, for ever. The Spirit of Truth is our guide in all the realms of Truth – explaining the Bible, giving insight and hope in our personal circumstances and using pressures and doubts to mature our faith. The Spirit will break down wrong attitudes in our lives, melt our hearts, fill us with His power and mould us so that we become Christlike.

O that the Comforter would come!
Nor visit as a transient guest,
But fix in me His constant home,
And take possession of my breast.

Charles Wesley

*   *   *

24th April

Jesus said: 'Let the little children come to me, and do not hinder them, for the kingdom of heaven belongs to such as these.'

Matthew 19:14

Kenneth Lysons wrote: 'Jesus did not equate childlikeness with childishness. Childlikeness refers to those qualities of children such as wonder and trust, which in later life can make adults winsome and attractive. Childishness relates to those aspects of childish behaviour that must be temporarily tolerated in the hope that with growing maturity they will be left behind. The development of Christian character entails blending adult strength and wisdom with childlike trust, wonder and singlemindedness.' In his letters to the Corinthian churches, Paul says believers start out as 'mere infants in Christ'. But the closer we are prepared to come to Jesus, the more our faith will grow into maturity. Then we shall have a faith full of wonder, love and praise.

When I was a child, I talked like a child, I thought like a child, I reasoned like a child. When I became a man, I put childish ways behind me. Now we see but a poor reflection; then we shall see face to face.

1 Corinthians 13:14

*   *   *

25th April

When you sow, you do not plant the body that will be, but just a seed, perhaps of corn or something else. But God gives it a body as He has determined...

1 Corinthians 15:37

I have come across an anonymous American poem which sheds a new light on the thought of death. Let me share it with you:

I have seen death too often to believe in death.
It is not an ending, but a withdrawal.
As one who finished a long journey
Stills the motor, turns off the lights,
Steps from the car
And walks up the path to the home that awaits...

Lord, I do not understand death – but I know that in the midst of life there is death all around. When death comes for friends, stop me from being 'holy' about it all; give me supportive words to say and helpful things to do. May each experience of death enrich our lives and deepen our faith in Jesus, who is the Resurrection and the Life.

*　　*　　*

26th April

Wanting to release Jesus, Pilate appealed to the crowd again. But they kept shouting, 'Crucify him! Crucify him!'

Luke 23:20

As a small boy attending Sunday School and singing in the choir, I remember lessons and sermons contrasting the crowds on Palm Sunday and Good Friday and speaking of the fickleness of human nature which could wave palm branches on the first occasion shouting 'Hosanna!' and on the second, pressuring the Roman Governor with loud shouting, 'Crucify him! Crucify him!' It was not till years later that I realised that the two crowds were not the same or that Jesus was not just a good-natured man falling into the hands of unscrupulous opponents, but a gentle and determinedly strong man challenging the rulers in their headquarters in Jerusalem and at the same time showing the peaceful, loving, forgiving nature of God.'

George Appleton

O Lord, once lifted on the glorious tree,
As Thou hast promised, draw men unto Thee:
Lift high the Cross, the love of Christ proclaim
Till all the world adore His sacred name.

M. R. Newbolt

*   *   *

27th April

'These commandments that I give you today are to be upon your hearts.'

Deuteronomy 6:6

Charles Haddon Spurgeon once wrote: 'It is blessed to eat into the very soul of the Bible until, at last, you come to talk in Scriptural language, and your spirit is flavoured with the words of the Lord, so that your blood is Bibline and the very essence of the Bible flows from you.' If that kind of Bible-saturation sounds unattainable, just think of the people you know whose only line of conversation is money or gossip about somebody else or football or royalty...! It is truly amazing what the mind can retain once motivated. It is truly a miracle what the heart can achieve when fed with the life-blood of God's holy law.

Help us O Lord, to learn
The truths your word imparts,
To study, that Your laws may be
Inscribed upon our hearts.

William W. Reid

*   *   *

28th April

Do not conform any longer to the pattern of this world, but be transformed by the renewing of your mind. Then you will be able to test and approve what God's will is – His good, pleasing and perfect will. For by the grace given me I say to every one of you: Do not think of yourself more highly than you ought, but rather think of yourself with sober judgement, in accordance with the measure of faith God has given you. Just as each of us has one body with many members, and these members do not all have the same function, so in Christ we who are many form one body, and each member belongs to all the others. We have different gifts, according to the grace given us. If a man's gift is prophesying, let him use it in proportion to his faith. If it is serving, let him serve; if it is teaching, let him teach; if it is encouraging, let him encourage; if it is contributing to the needs of others, let him give generously; if it is leadership, let him govern diligently; if it is showing mercy, let him do it cheerfully.

Romans 12:2-9

*   *   *

29th April

And the Lord God formed man from the dust of the ground and breathed into his nostrils the breath of life...

Genesis 2:7

Every breath I take says - I love You
And every beat of my heart says - I'm Yours.
Every step that I take says - I need You
And I will bless Your Holy name.

You are my Redeemer, the reason that I live,
Yes, and You are my salvation
And I will bless Your holy name.

Every day that goes by shows Your mercy,
And every gift that You give shows You care.
Every song that I sing says - You are worthy
And I will bless Your Holy name.

Eddie Espinosa

Jesus said: 'Peace be with you. As the Father has sent me, I am sending you.' And with that He breathed on them and said: 'Receive the Holy Spirit.' Lord Jesus, I ask You to breathe on me now... and through the Holy Spirit I will breathe Your love.

*   *   *

30th April

O Lord, you have searched me and know me... you have laid your hand upon me. Such knowledge is too wonderful for me.

Psalm 139: 1, 5–6

In our world today there is a constant demand that everything be made understandable. There are *Teach Yourself* books on everything from motor mechanics to Greek. Our society is geared to either dissecting and proving things or else despising and rejecting them. What a sad mistake this attitude is. Oh for the psalmist's humble, loving acceptance of the fact that we can never reduce God to our level. Carlo Carretto wrote: 'God is simple and we make Him complicated. He is close to us and we make Him far away... The true secret of making contact with God is littleness, simplicity of heart, poverty of spirit: all the things that pride, wealth and cleverness foil in us.' Yes, after all, if love could be measured, that would mean it had a limit – and God's love has no limit.

Lord, teach me to praise You. Let me see in the vast universe around me Your strength and power... I can't begin to understand... but I can touch, and feel the warmth. Lord, let that be enough.

Eddie Askew

* * *

1st May

Christ is all, and is in all.

Colossians 3:11

As the bridegroom to his chosen, as the king unto his realm,
As the keep unto the castle, as the pilot to the helm,
So, Lord, art Thou to me.

As the fountain in the garden, as the candle in the dark,
As the treasure in the coffer, as the manna in the ark,
So, Lord, art Thou to me.

As the music at the banquet, as the stamp unto the seal,
As the med'cine to the fainting, as the wine cup at the meal,
    So, Lord, art Thou to me.

As the ruby in the setting, as the honey in the comb,
As the light within the lantern, as the father in the home,
    So, Lord, art Thou to me.

           John Tauler (paraphrased by Emma Bevan)

Dear Lord, I praise You today, for I realise that You are truly in all I see and touch, and that You are truly all I need and all I have. Thine be the glory!

*   *   *

2nd May

Jesus said: 'This is how you should pray: "Our Father, hallowed be Your name..." '

           Matthew 6:9

One of the greatest hindrances to Christianity has been the tendency of some people in every generation to make it a 'me and God' affair. It is a 'me and God and you' situation. Historically, Christianity holds in tension the ultimate importance of the individual and the corporate nature of the body of Christ. At the time Jesus taught this prayer to His followers, it may have been somewhat easier for them to understand the meaning of the word 'our' than it is for us today. The Western world thinks individually first, and then corporately; but this was not true in the world of Jesus' time. The Jew was a member of a people first, and then an individual.

        Chuck and Anne Murphy (*Bold to Say 'Our Father'*)

    Father in heaven, grant to your children
    Mercy and blessing, song never ceasing.
    Love to unite us – grace to redeem us,
    Father in heaven, Father our God.
        Daniel Thambyrajah Niles (Sri Lanka)

*   *   *

3rd May

Jesus said: 'The eye is the lamp of your body. If your eyes
are good, your whole body will be full of light.'

Matthew 6:22

What does this mean? If your 'eye' – your outlook on life,
your whole way of looking at things and people – is generous,
then your whole personality is illumined or lit up. Jesus had
little money to give, but He was generous towards all – the
sick, the needy, the maimed, the sinful and the unlovely. His
whole personality was full of light. So be like Jesus – begin to
see everybody and everything with a generous 'eye'. Don't
be a mean person. One of the greatest definitions of
Christianity I have ever heard is simply this: Give, give,
give, give, give...

*Lord, I have been mean and ungracious in Your sight – I have given little but have
expected much. My life has been dull, my attitude stiff and uncaring. Lord, change
me.*

*　　　*　　　*

4th May

Jesus said: 'For who is greater, the one who is at the table
or the one who serves? But I am among you as one who
serves.'

Luke 22:27

I don't believe it matters to God or the world whether a man
is a butcher or a bishop. It matters whether he is a good
butcher or a good bishop... for all service to the community
is service to God. This indeed is the best way we can serve
God. 'Divine Service', so called, is only the preparation for
the true divine service which is interpreting the Spirit of
Christ in terms of your own job. And a man's work for God
should not be just his church work, which is a very small

percentage of his time. It should be his business, which he should regard as his first contribution to the Kingdom of God... No, it is not the job, but the spirit in which the job is done which determines whether work is sacred or secular!

Dr Leslie Weatherhead

Jesus calls us!
By Thy mercies, Saviour, may we hear Thy call,
Give our hearts to Thine obedience,
Serve and love Thee best of all.

Cecil F. Alexander

*   *   *

5th May

I pray that you, being rooted and established in love, may have power, together with all the saints, to grasp how wide and how long and high and deep is the love of Christ, and to know this love that surpasses knowledge – that you may be filled to the measure of all the fullness of God.

Now to Him who is able to do immeasurably more than all we ask or imagine, according to His power that is at work within us, to Him be glory in the church and in Christ Jesus throughout all generations, for ever and ever...

I urge you to live a life worthy of the calling you have received. Be completely humble and gentle; be patient, bearing with one another in love. Make every effort to keep the unity of the Spirit through the bond of peace. There is one body and one Spirit – just as you were called to one hope, when you were called – one Lord, one faith, one baptism; one God and Father of all who is over all and through all and in all.

Ephesians 3:17–20; 4:1–6

*   *   *

6th May

> John said: 'I baptise you with water for repentance. But
> after me will come one who is more powerful than I... He
> will baptise you with the Holy Spirit and with fire.'
>
> Matthew 3:11

John the Baptist seems to shine out of the pages of the New
Testament with a two-fold light. He knew himself to be the
messenger – the forerunner – the voice of which Isaiah had
spoken, crying in the wilderness, 'Prepare the way for the
Lord.' He knew that his role was only to arouse the people to
recognise their need of repentance and to outwardly express
their commitment to a new way of life by being baptised. He
also realised that the one to follow him, God's Messiah,
would not only baptise but would through the power of the
Holy Spirit purge and transform lives so that they would
never be the same again. The world would never be the same
again!

Lord forgive me that I am so occupied with my own need
for forgiveness that I forget the world. Your Holy Spirit is for
all who turn to Jesus... for all who repent... And help me,
once baptised to new life, to lift my eyes and hands to the
challenge of those in my neighbourhood, with their silent and
secret needs.

O Lord, baptise our hearts into a sense of the conditions and need of all men.
George Fox, founder of the Society
of Friends (Quakers)

* * *

7th May

> Jesus said: 'Do not leave Jerusalem, but wait for the gift
> my Father promised, which you have heard me speak
> about... In a few days you will be baptised with the Holy
> Spirit... You will receive power when the Holy Spirit
> comes on you; and you will be my witnesses in Jerusalem,

and in all Judea and Samaria, and to the ends of the earth.'

After He said this, He was taken up before their very eyes, and a cloud hid him from their sight.

They were looking intently up into the sky as He was going, when suddenly two men dressed in white stood beside them. 'Men of Galilee,' they said, 'why do you stand there looking into the sky? This same Jesus, who has been taken from you into heaven, will come back in the same way you have seen Him go into heaven.'

Acts 1:4–12

* * *

8th May

I will give you a new heart and put a new spirit in you; I will remove from you your heart of stone and give you a heart of flesh.

Ezekiel 36:26

O for a heart to praise my God...
O for a heart set free from all that is sinful.
Lord, I pray for a heart that is submissive and meek –
A heart where only Christ is heard to speak
And where He reigns supreme.
I long for a lowly, contrite heart,
A heart that is believing, true and clean.
I need a heart where every thought is renewed and filled with love;
I pray that it will grow daily more like the heart of Jesus.
Lord, write Your name on my heart...
It is the dearest and the best name...
The name of Love.

adapted from Charles Wesley

O Lord Jesus Christ, take us in Thy care... purify our hearts and souls, keep clean our bodies, that in all we may please Thee, sleeping or waking, for ever. Amen.

Christian Prayers (1566)

* * *

9th May

Jesus was taken before their eyes, and a cloud hid Him
from their sight.

Acts 1:9

Between our Lord's resurrection and His ascension there
were forty days during which He 'showed Himself alive' to
His disciples. A remarkable phenomenon of those forty days
was that our Lord, instead of remaining continuously visible
to the disciples, communicated with them in a series of
sudden appearances separated by intervals of invisibility.
Why was this? It was to teach them that when He was not
visible He was none the less present. In His sudden
appearances He gave evidence that He had heard all their
conversations during His invisibility, as when He appeared
and tenderly chided doubting Thomas, thereby indicating
that although unseen, He had heard Thomas' words. The
centre point of all was that during those forty days they had
learned the transforming truth of His invisible presence with
them.

J. Sidlow Baxter from Awake My Heart

Alleluia! Not as orphans are we left in sorrow now;
Alleluia! He is near us, faith believes, not questions how;
Though the cloud from sight received Him
When the forty days were o'er
Shall our hearts forget His promise, 'I am with you evermore.'
William Chatterton Dix

*   *   *

10th May

You say, 'I am rich; I have acquired wealth and do not
need a thing.' But you do not realise that you are
wretched, poor, blind and naked.

Revelation 3:17

Shortly after the death of her husband a widow went to stay for a weekend with her sister and brother-in-law. On the Sunday morning she asked if they would go with her to the local church. 'Oh no,' they said. 'We don't need that sort of thing.' Saint John the Divine's vision of the complacent church at Laodicea leaps from the page. How very modern it all sounds! How the majority of people today pooh-pooh worship – every conceivable distraction is put before God. And yet Christ still stands at the door and waits. He stands at the door of complacent churches as well as at the door of complacent hearts, offering Himself. Lord, in my need, I beg You to come into my heart and life.

> *Just as I am, poor wretched, blind,*
> *Sight, riches, healing of the mind –*
> *Yea, all I need, in Thee to find,*
> *O Lamb of God, I come.*

Charlotte Elliott

* * *

11th May

> But a Samaritan, as he travelled, came where the man was; and when he saw him he took pity on him. He went to him and bandaged his wounds...
>
> Luke 10:33

A friend and I were considering life and its purpose. I said, even with increasing paralysis and loss of speech, I believed there was a purpose for my life, but I was not sure what it was at that particular time. We agreed to pray about it for a week. I was then sure that my present purpose is simply to receive other people's prayers and kindness and to link together all those who are lovingly concerned about me, many of whom are unknown to one another. After a while my friend said: 'It must be hard to be the wounded Jew, when, by nature, you would rather be the Good Samaritan.' It is hard! It would be unbearable were it not for my belief that the wounded man and the Samaritan are inseperable. It was the helplessness of the one that brought out the best in the other and linked them together.

Enid Henke, who died a month after she wrote this

* * *

12th May

But whatever was to my profit I now consider loss for the sake of Christ... I consider everything a loss compared to the surpassing greatness of knowing Christ Jesus my Lord, for whose sake I have lost all things. I consider them rubbish, that I may gain Christ and be found in Him, not having a righteousness of my own that comes from the law, but that which is through faith in Christ – the righteousness that comes from God and is by faith. I want to know Christ and the power of His resurrection and the fellowship of sharing in His sufferings, becoming like Him in His death, and so, somehow, to attain to the resurrection from the dead... I press on to take hold of that for which Christ Jesus took hold of me... Forgetting what is behind and straining towards what is ahead, I press on towards the goal to win the prize for which God has called me heavenwards in Christ Jesus.

Philippians 3:7–14

* * *

13th May

Simeon said: 'This child is destined to cause the falling and rising of many in Israel... and a sword will pierce your own soul too.'

Luke 2:35

Mary, the mother of God... Mary, not much more than a girl, and yet representing motherhood... And surely we see in Mary all the undeserved suffering of motherhood. We look in on her story as we would watch a TV 'soap' – we know what is coming to Mary, but we don't know what is coming to us. Lord, I pray now for the mothers of children with handicaps, for mothers who find out that their children have been stealing, lying, being violent... I pray for mothers whose children go to borstal and to prison, to psychiatric hospitals and to drug rehabilitation centres. Uphold and strengthen women in their burden of caring, nursing and loving. Lord, strengthen me.

Thank You, Lord, for the love of mothers and of those who love in place of mothers.

* * *

14th May

Jesus said: 'Every day I was with you, teaching in the temple courts, and you did not arrest me.' Then everyone deserted Him and fled.

Mark 14:50

Jesus must have been so disappointed by His disciples – when He needed them they disappeared, they evaporated into the darkness of the garden of Gethsemane. But it was not only long ago that Jesus suffered disappointment. Today it is the same – innumerable disciples are deserting Him. In 'religious' conflicts around the world people who call themselves Christians are degrading and blaspheming Him.

Lord, I know that I too have been a disappointment – I have grieved Your love and wounded those I love. Grant that I may live to bring joy and comfort by my dedication to Your will. Help me to stand the many tests of each day in close obedience to Your commandments.

Whosoever is daily prepared to lose his life will be faithful to Jesus in the time of trial and will be able to give his life for Him.

Text on the wall opposite the entrance
to the Garden of Gethsemane

* * *

15th May

God made the wild animals according to their kinds, the
livestock according to their kinds, and all the creatures
that move along the ground... and God saw that it was
good.

Genesis 1:25

As far back as I can remember I was saddened by the amount
of misery I saw in the world around me. One thing that
especially saddened me was that unfortunate animals had to
suffer much pain and misery. It was quite incomprehensible
to me why in my evening prayers I should pray for human
beings only. So when my mother had prayed with me and
kissed me good night, I used to add silently a prayer that I
had composed myself for all living creatures: O heavenly
Father, protect and bless all things that have breath: guard
them from all evil and let them sleep in peace.

Albert Schweitzer

He prayeth best who loveth best
All things both great and small;
For the dear God who loveth us,
He made and loveth all.

Coleridge

*　　*　　*

16th May

Joseph had a dream... He said to his brothers: 'Listen to
this dream...'

Genesis: 37:5

Joseph has not been alone – we thank God that people in all
generations have had dreams of a world that could and
should be. Here is a dream written by John Page of Alaska:

I have a dream of a church which is a caring church:
whose congregation is drawn from many races, nations, ages, social backgrounds

92

and exhibits the unity and diversity of the family of God;
whose fellowship is warm and welcoming;
whose members love one another with a pure heart, forebearing one another,
forgiving one another and bearing one another's burdens;
which offers friendship to the lonely, support to the weak,
and acceptance to those who are despised and rejected by society,
whose love spills over to the world outside, attractive, infectious,
irresistible... the love of Christ Himself.

Lord, as I make this my dream too, help me to busy myself to make this dream come true.

* * *

17th May

When Jesus came out wearing the crown of thorns and
the purple robe, Pilate said to them: 'Here is the man!'

John 19:5

How often in the stress of our daily living we need the comfort of a fellow human being – Wesley reminds us that there is no such thing as 'isolated Christianity'. There are limits, however, to the most sincere human effort. Nevertheless, Christianity is supreme in all facets of life, for where other religions and cults rely on the teaching of its leader, Christianity, first and foremost, is a relationship with a person. Jesus Christ is absolutely vital to our faith. We all need to 'Behold the man'. Our risen Lord ministers Calvary love to all who call on Him.

Raymond Haley

Behold, the Lamb of God...
Sinners believe the gospel word,
Jesus is come, your soul to save...

Charles Wesley

* * *

18th May

They saw what seemed to be tongues of fire that separated and came to rest on each of them. All of them were filled with the Holy Spirit...

Acts 2:3–4

For all the blessings and needs we have named, and the many more unamed but known to you, God we thank You and pray that You hear us when we call on You. O God, we pray You, fill Your servants with Your Holy Spirit, that the works we undertake may be redemptive, our words prophetic and our worship meaningful. Inspire us with Your love, challenge us with Your truth and empower us with Your strength. Amen.

Mercy A. Oduyoye (WCC)

> *Fire of the Spirit – moving and loving –*
> *Warm us and lead us, encourage and change us.*
> *Fire of the Spirit – give light to our chaos,*
> *Drive out our confusions and heal our hurt world.*
> *Fire of the Spirit – join us together,*
> *Dance in our churches, transform our lives.*

From Catch the Flame MCOD (HMD)

*   *   *

19th May

Then Peter stood up with the Eleven, raised his voice and addressed the crowd: 'Fellow-Jews and all of you who are in Jerusalem, let me explain this to you; listen carefully to what I say. These men are not drunk, as you suppose. It's only nine in the morning! No, this is what was spoken by the prophet Joel:

In the last days, God says,
I will pour out my Spirit on all people.
Your sons and daughters will prophesy,
your young men will see visions,

94

your old men will dream dreams.
Even on my servants, both men and women,
I will pour out my Spirit in those days,
and they will prophesy.
I will show wonders in the heaven above
and signs on the earth below,
blood and fire and billows of smoke.
The sun will be turned to darkness
and the moon to blood
before the coming of the great and glorious day of the Lord.
And everyone who calls on the name of the Lord will be saved.'

Acts 2:14–21

* * *

20th May

Jesus took bread, gave thanks and broke it, and gave it to
His disciples, saying, 'Take it; this is my body.'

Mark 14:22

For years I happily sang Pastor Iverson's gentle chorus, *Spirit of the Living God* with reverence and sincerity, but with not the slightest idea of what the words actually meant. It's so easy to sing 'Break me, melt me, mould me, fill me...' It sounds so 'right'. Only when I experienced the devastating agony of bereavement did I understand what it was to be broken. My pride and confidence were totally smashed – I was emotionally shattered. Only when we have nothing, when we are emptied of self and reaching out for God, can the Holy Spirit fill us. As Jesus broke the bread for His disciples, He was aware of the correlation between the bread and His own body – both had to be broken in order to be shared. Being broken by the power of the Holy Spirit is not negative but positive – we are not broken to be thrown away as useless, but we are broken to be re-made, to be made useful, to be filled with the Spirit of the Living Jesus.

Spirit of the Living God, fall afresh on me,
Break me – break down wrong attitudes;
Melt me – melt my hard heart;

95

Mould me – mould my life to be like Jesus;
Fill me – fill me afresh with His power in my life.

* * *

21st May

On hearing His words, some of the people said, 'Surely
this man is the Prophet.' Others said, 'He is the Christ.'
Still others asked, 'How can the Christ come from
Galilee?'

John 7:41–42

Not surprisingly, people couldn't make their minds up about
Jesus. It seems much the same with any public figure – there
is never unanimous agreement as to whether they are
marvellous or useless. There are as many opinions as people!
Some men and woman endure torture and death for their
opinions and deeply held faith, whilst others never bother to
think about Jesus enough to even have a firm idea of who He
was or is.

Lord, may I always ask questions – always seek deeper
understanding. I can never embrace all Your truth in this
life, but give me an openness of mind so that I may draw as
close as I possibly can to the prophet from Galilee... the
Christ – the Messiah.

Who is He in yonder stall, at whose feet the shepherds fall?
Who is He in deep distress, fasting in the wilderness?
Who is He that from the grave comes to heal and help and save?
'Tis the Lord! The King of Glory!

B. R. Hanby

* * *

22nd May

For since the creation of the world God's invisible
qualities – His eternal power and divine nature – have
been clearly seen... so that men are without any excuse.

Romans 1:20

I love You Lord, not with doubt in my heart but with blessed assurance. With Your Word You struck my heart, and I loved You. At every turn the heavens and the earth, all wonders and creatures made me love You... There is no excuse for me to ever stop loving You. But what is it that I love? I love a kind of light, a melody of fragrance, a kind of food and a way of embracing when I love my God. And this embracing, fragrance, food, melody and light of my inner soul shines in my heart, sounds in my mind, tastes in my senses and stays with me in such a way that I am never satisfied, but long for more of this experience. This is what I love when I love my God.

Freely adapted from St Augustine

God is love. Whoever lives in love lives in God, and God in him... There is no fear in love... We love because He first loved us.

1 John 4:16, 18, 19

* * *

23rd May

Are they ashamed of their loathsome conduct? No, they have no shame at all; they do not even know how to blush.

Jeremiah 6:15

I know it is an English translation, but what a superb turn of phrase the prophet Jeremiah used! And his indignant rebuke to the greedy, the lecherous, the deceivers and the other evildoers could today be a condemnation of many a television programme, video, magazine or piece of political wangling. Nothing is new. However, the vast majority of the general public carries on in the hope that things will turn out right in the end. Perhaps we who note the plunging barometer of anti-social behaviour should have more courage to say outright that mankind is at the crossroads, that things are *not* all right. Men, women and even children are in deep despair – broken by crises, struggling against evil. There is no peace in their minds, hearts or countries. Lord, why am I complacent? Why am I silent? Have I too forgotten how to blush?

This is what the Lord says: 'Stand at the crossroads and look; ask for the ancient paths, ask where the good way is, and walk in it, and you will find rest for your souls.

Jeremiah 6:16

* * *

24th May

They asked each other: 'Were not our hearts burning within us while He talked with us on the road and opened the Scriptures to us?'

Luke 24:31

In his book, *It was on a Monday Morning*, the late Rev John Jackson wrote a page or two on central heating. He mentioned John Wesley, who on 24th May 1738 had had a heart-warming experience of Jesus Christ, and he also wrote about the two on the Emmaus road whose hearts had burned. He said, 'The reason for the heart-warming – the central heating – was Jesus... Once you let Jesus come to live and to rule your heart, you find your heart is strangely warmed and life is never the same again. No matter how cold may be the icy blasts of circumstances, nor how freezing and chilly may be events or people, you have this inner glow that Jesus brings with Him to everybody who will receive Him. I hope this is the kind of central heating you've got.'

Drawn to the cross of Christ the Lord
And by the Spirit's voice informed;
Trusting the Master's assuring word
The wakening heart feels strangely warmed.
Decisive this transforming hour
For all who know God's saving power!

David Mowbray

* * *

25th May

Be joyful in hope, patient in affliction, faithful in prayer.
Share with God's people who are in need.

Romans 12:12–13

This prayer was written by a Chinese Christian: 'We praise Thee, our Father, that even in the hour of darkness we can come to Thee with confidence and unflinching faith... Help us, Father, to learn the lessons that have come out of conflict; help us to work for the new day that will bring us one step nearer to Thy Kingdom. Grant that the day may not be too far off when the nations will become one, when war will be abolished, and we shall all live peacefully together in one holy family.'

Lord, I give thanks for the witness of Christians in China and Hong Kong. From their affliction and conflicts may I learn a deeper meaning of faithfulness in prayer. Bless us all with hope, patience and joy.

May we, like the Samaritan, not fail in the oil of comfort, the wine of justice, the involvement of the patient mule and the generosity which, having given, promises more, until the caring is complete.

A Prayer from Hong Kong

* * *

26th May

How great is the love the Father has lavished on us, that we should be called children of God! And that is what we are! The reason the world does not know us is that it did not know Him. Dear friends, now we are children of God, and what we will be has not yet been made known. But we know that when He appears, we shall be like Him, for we shall see Him as He is. Everyone who has this hope in Him purifies himself, just as He is pure.

Everyone who sins breaks the law; in fact, sin is lawlessness. But you know that He appeared so that He might take away our sins. And in Him is no sin. No-one who lives in Him keeps on sinning. No-one who continues to sin has either seen Him or known Him...

No-one who is born of God will continue to sin, because God's seed remains in him; he cannot go on sinning, because he has been born of God. This is how we know who the children of God are... Anyone who does not do what is right is not a child of God; neither is any one who does not love his brother.

1 John 3:1–6, 9–10

* * *

27th May

Flowers appear on the earth; the season of singing has come... The fig-tree forms its early fruit; the blossoming vines spread their fragrance.

Song of Songs 2:12–13

They're so delicate, Lord, the flowers You made,
a mind-stunning assortment of shapes, and forms and colours;
an emotionally-nourishing variety of perfumes and textures;
a source of pleasure, and stimulation and healing – and yet –
They are trodden underfoot; attacked by frosts, and diseases and pests,
they are pulled up, cut down, dried, pressed and crushed...
We humans seem to have made a virtue of strength;
to have placed a high value on a thick skin,
whereas, like the flowers You made, Your nature was seen at its best
when You had been exposed to injury, and hostility, and death.
If you consider it necessary, Lord,
teach me how to be vulnerable.

Gordon Bailey

The fruit-trees in their seasons and the vine,
The sycamore, the cedar, and the palm,
The lotus and the orchid and the rose
Praise and reflect the beauty of Christ.

J. P. McAuley

* * *

28th May

Leaving the crowd behind, they took Him along in the
boat... a furious squall came up, and the waves broke
over the boat, so that it was nearly swamped.

Mark 4:36-37

We are labouring at the oars, most of us, struggling against a
head wind to keep our sense of direction. Natural
surroundings and our own weaknesses are too much for us.
We are helpless, at the mercy of the storms of temptation,
emotional distraction, doubt, worry, disillusionment,
bereavement. They come down on us without warning and
drive us off course. And that is hard when we are known for
Christians and supposed to be ready for everything that
comes. When that happens all the calm beauty of the
spiritual life seems a long way away. And it is just then,
above all other times, that the miracle of prayer happens.

Evelyn Underhill

So, when our life is clouded o'er,
And storm-winds drift us from the shore,
Say, lest we sink to rise no more: 'Peace, be still!'

Godfrey Thring

*   *   *

29th May

This is what the Lord says to the House of Israel: 'Seek
me and live.'

Amos 5:4

Amos spoke out the word of the Lord to the people. By and
large the prophets were pretty unpopular because their
integrity prevented them from placating the kings or
flattering the priests or watering down the truth for general
consumption. Lord, help me to be aware that the prophets
did indeed speak Your words. Jesus Christ came into the
world to speak and to live Your word, and by Your Holy

Spirit He is still speaking to this world – and to me. May Your word bring power and comfort and eternal life to those whom I lift before You in prayer.

God has spoken by His prophets, spoken His unchanging word:
Each from age to age proclaiming God, the one, the righteous Lord.
God has spoken by Christ Jesus...
Light from Light to earth descending, Man, revealing God to man.
God is speaking by His Spirit...
God still speaks, His word unchanging, God the first and God the Last.

George W. Briggs

*　　*　　*

30th May

The boundary lines have fallen for me in pleasant places;
surely I have a delightful inheritance.

Psalm 16:6

Today, Lord, I want to thank You for where I live, for the pleasantness of my surroundings and for the happy times I have with my family and friends. It is sometimes refreshing to look at my surroundings through the eyes of a 'visitor' who is looking for good things, rather than through my eyes, which are dulled by familiarity. Lord, I do feel blessed – and truly, my heart feels better for praising instead of moaning... And when I am in this receptive attitude I realise that not only have I to be thankful for where I live, but also my heart should overflow with joy and gratitude for the grace by which I live. Lord of my life, Heavenly Father of all, I bring my praise in Jesus' name.

I pray also that the eyes of your heart may be enlightened in order that you may know the hope to which He has called you, the riches of His glorious inheritance in the saints, and His incomparably great power for us who believe.

Ephesians 1:18–19

*　　*　　*

31st May

If you do not stand firm in your faith, you will not stand
at all.

Isaiah 7:9

Sometimes life can chug along in routine contentment, but at
other times it can be frustrating, or empty of any meaning –
it can be up and down with such speed that we can be left
reeling in emotional and spiritual shock. We may say, 'We
don't know what's hit us'... and in the shadowy hours of our
upheaval we are apt to find our faith faltering. Yet faith will
be all the stronger for being tested – we are shaken, yes, but if
our foundation is firm, we shall stand up to the trials ahead.
The Spirit of God is with us: this is our faith in the One who
is beyond understanding. In the words of Karl Barth, 'You
are on firm ground only when your allegiance is given clearly
and unequivocally to Jesus Christ.' Lord, deepen my faith
today.

*So then, just as you received Christ Jesus our Lord, continue to live in Him, rooted
and built up in Him, strengthened in the faith as you were taught, and overflowing
with thankfulness.*

Colossians 2:6–7

*   *   *

1st June

Abraham planted a tamarisk tree in Beersheba, and there
he called upon the name of the Lord, the Eternal God.

Genesis 21:33

Here we are back to basics – hundreds of years before the
building of the temple, Abraham worshipped God out in the
open. The story is told of a venerable bishop who was invited
to the grand opening ceremony of a brand new church.
When he got to the doors he stood still in dismay and said he
couldn't go in. He said the church was too full – too full of

people's ideas and expectations and demands. He could not reach God inside that building.

Lord, I want to feel anew a sense of awe in the countryside, at the park, by the river-bank and in the garden. Uncluttered by any man-made attempts at worship, I want to whisper Your name beneath a tree, to gaze up to the sky and be thankful, to stop and feel the sun on my face and know Your peace.

> *I come to the garden alone*
> *While the dew is still on the roses;*
> *And the voice I hear, falling on my ear,*
> *The Son of God discloses:*
> *And He walks with me, and He talks with me and He tells me I am His own.*
>
> C. Austin Miles

*   *   *

2nd June

Once when we were going to the place of prayer, we were met by a slave girl who had a spirit by which she predicted the future. She earned a great deal of money for her owners by fortune-telling. This girl followed Paul and the rest of us, shouting, 'These men are servants of the Most High God, who are telling you the way to be saved.' She kept this up for many days. Finally, Paul became so troubled that he turned round and said to the spirit, 'In the name of Jesus Christ I command you to come out of her!' At that moment the spirit left her.

When the owners of the slave girl realised that their hope of making money was gone, they seized Paul and Silas and dragged them into the market-place to face the authorities. They brought them before the magistrates and said: 'These men are Jews, and are throwing our city into an uproar by advocating customs unlawful for us Romans to accept or practise.'

The crowd joined in the attack against Paul and Silas, and the migistrates ordered them to be stripped and beaten.

Acts 16:15–22

*   *   *

3rd June

Let us draw near to God with a sincere heart in full
assurance of faith...

Hebrews 10:22

Blessed assurance, Jesus is mine:
O what a foretaste of glory divine!
Heir of salvation, purchase of God;
Born of His Spirit, washed in His blood.

Perfect submission, perfect delight,
Visions of rapture burst on my sight;
Angels descending, bring from above
Echoes of mercy – whispers of love.

Perfect submission, all is at rest,
I in my Saviour am happy and blest;
Watching and waiting, looking above,
Filled with His goodness, lost in His love.

This is my story, this is my song,
Praising my Saviouir all the day long.

Frances van Alstyne

To Thee, O God, we turn for peace... but grant us too the
blessed assurance that nothing shall deprive us of that peace,
neither ourselves, nor our foolish earthly desires, nor my
wild longings, nor the anxious cravings of my heart.

Soren Kierkegaard

* * *

4th June

The whole assembly became silent as they listened to
Barnabas and Paul telling about the miraculous signs and
wonders God had done among the Gentiles through
them.

Acts 15:12

William Temple said, 'It is not ourselves, but our witness to Christ for which we want to claim attention. Never mind who or what I am, but do listen when I speak to you of Christ.' Perhaps we Christians we do not take the opportunities given to us to speak about Christ – we are afraid of being labelled 'religious nuts'. Yet people are surprisingly ready to listen to an account of a personal experience of guidance or a miracle. They urgently want to know about a Saviour who is not locked away within the pages of the Holy Scripture and whom they can relate to and lean on in the day-to-day concerns of living. Lord, give me courage today to encourage someone else through what You have done for me.

Paul was preaching the good news about Jesus and the resurrection. Then they took him and brought him to a meeting of the Areopagus, where they said to him, 'May we know what this new teaching is that you are presenting? You are bringing some strange ideas to our ears and we want to know what they mean.'

Acts 17:19–20

*   *   *

5th June

For I am the Lord, your God, who takes hold of your
right hand and says to you, 'Do not fear; I will help you.'
Isaiah 41:13

On my walks I've come across groups of young people absailing. It all looks amazingly dramatic, but I can't imagine myself disappearing over the edge of some cliff, my life depending on a mere length of rope! To the enthusiast, however, absailing is fun. Each to their own!

When watching these adventures, I can't help but think how we each need to put our trust in God in the same way as the absailers give their trust to their leader – the one who holds them safe. Many experiences in life make us feel as though we are going over a cliff, but God has promised that

He will help us, He will hold us. Jesus said: 'Trust in God, trust also in me.' Lord, I lift my open hands to You... Even as I breathe my prayer, I trust in Your saving power.

> *Father, I place into Your hands my friends and family –*
> *Father, I place into Your hands the things that trouble me:*
> *Father, I place into Your hands the person I would be,*
> *For I know I always can trust You.*

> *J. Hewer*

*   *   *

6th June

Now that same day two of them were going to a village called Emmaus, about seven miles from Jerusalem.

Luke 24:13

For many the story of the Emmaus road is a favourite. I can so easily see myself in that situation, caught up in my own concerns and oblivious to anyone around me. Frank Topping has put it like this: 'Lord, how often have I walked the Emmaus road in your company and not seen You? How often has my myopic faith looked at the pilgrim Christ and perceived only a sympathetic traveller? How often have I been deaf to words of love and healing, been within reach of touching the hem of the robe of the risen Christ and in utter self-assurance, unaware of my blindness, ignored the pierced hand stretched out for me?'

When He was at the table with them, He took bread, gave thanks, broke it and began to give it to them. Then their eyes were open and they recognised Him...

Luke 24:30

*   *   *

7th June

I will put my Spirit in you and you will live.

Ezekiel 37:14

These words of the Sovereign Lord spoken through the prophet Ezekiel are found at the end of the vision of the dry bones. Although it is commonly associated with catchy spiritual, *'Dem bones, dem bones, dem dry bones...'* it is nevertheless a potent picture of the transformation which God can bring about in a life. God's breath, His life-giving Spirit, can come into our lives, course through our being, revive dry relationships, restore dying marriages and give new meaning and purpose to our very existence. God does not mean you to be lifeless – He doesn't want you to feel useless. He waits to give you His Spirit so that today, even now, you will feel your heart warmed and will rejoice with new enthusiasm, faith and trust. Lord, pour out Your spirit on me now.

> *Breathe on me breath of God,*
> *Fill me with life anew;*
> *Breathe on me breath of God*
> *Till I am wholly Thine...*

Edwin Hatch

* * *

8th June

> I kneel before the Father, from whom the whole family in
> heaven and on earth derives its name. I pray that out of
> His glorious riches He may strengthen you...
>
> Ephesians 3:15

The family which deludes itself into thinking that it will never have any problems is set for a rude awakening! There will be times in family life when there is a desperate need for strength. When things are collapsing around us, God's strength is the one strength which can hold us together. It is hardly any comfort to know about other people's troubles, or to realise that we are not the first or the last to have problems – but it is a comfort to turn and talk things through in prayer, on our knees... The Lord and Father of our Saviour Jesus Christ hears and answers prayer.

Abba, Father, help those who struggle with miserable circumstances, incompatibility, infidelity, brutality... rebellious and defiant children, economic worries... Comfort couples who are unable to have their own children... Guide those who are adopting or fostering... Let every marriage, every family, have its roots and foundations in Your love.

Joy Whyte

* * *

9th June

About midnight Paul and Silas were praying and singing hymns to God, and the other prisoners were listening to them. Suddenly there was such a violent earthquake that the foundations of the prison were shaken. At once all the prison doors flew open, and everybody's chains came loose. The jailer woke up, and when he saw the prison doors open, he drew his sword and was about to kill himself because he thought the prisoners had escaped. But Paul shouted; 'Don't harm yourself. We are all here!'

The jailer called for lights, rushed in and fell trembling before Paul and Silas. He brought them out and asked: 'Men, what must I do to be saved?'

They replied: 'Believe in the Lord Jesus, and you will be saved – you and your household.' Then they spoke the word of the Lord to him and to all the others in his house.

Acts 16:25–34

* * *

10th June

The desert and the parched land will be glad; the wilderness will rejoice and blossom. Like the crocus it will burst into bloom, it will rejoice greatly and shout for joy.

Isaiah 35:1

As we peered from the air-conditioned coach the countryside was barren and parched. Desert. Uninteresting brown! It went on for mile upon dry mile in the October heat. The courier cheerfully told us, 'If you'd come in March, you

109

would have seen grass and flowers everywhere!' It was very hard to believe. His words spoke to me about something which is even harder to believe: the reaility of resurrection and new life in Jesus Christ. Into barren, dusty lives comes an infusion of joy – a supernatural regeneration which cannot be contained. Jesus is alive! He transforms our attitude to death, He lifts us up to be changed with Him. But He doesn't say to us, 'Come back in March' – all He says is 'Come, follow me.'

> *I am the resurrection, I am the life.*
> *He who believes in me, even if he die, he shall live for ever.*
> *And I will raise him up,*
> *And I will raise him up, I will raise him up on the last day.*
> S. Suzanne Toolan

*   *   *

11th June

> There are different kinds of gifts, but the same Spirit.
> There are different kinds of service, but the same Lord.
> 1 Corinthians 12:4

One of the questions frequently asked by new Christians is this: 'Does the Holy Spirit dwell in me? And if so, how can I tell?' The evidence for His presence within is 'the fruit of the Spirit.'

Love: Am I able to show love to the people whom I would normally dislike?

Joy: Am I a happy Christian?

Peace: Am I secure and serene when things don't appear to be going right?

Long-suffering: Am I patient and able to bear with other people's faults and imperfections?

Kindness: Do I excel in the demonstration of kind and tender actions?

Goodness: It was said of Jesus that 'He went about doing good.' Do I?

Faithfulness: If my whole life suddenly crashed about me, would I still trust Him?

Meekness: Am I gentle in my rebukes, and Christlike in my judgements?

Temperance: Am I self-controlled in all things?

Taken from a church magazine

Lord, I have so much to learn. Give me the humility to examine my heart and my actions, and give me sincerity in seeking to make both more Christlike.

*   *   *

12th June

Jesus said: 'What goes into a man's mouth does not make him unclean, but what comes out of his mouth, that is what makes him unclean.'

Matthew 15:11

The story is told of the late Dr Sangster taking a walk along a beautiful avenue of trees. As he strolled he noticed that two of the trees were shrivelled, ugly and very dead. It turned out that a gas main which ran underneath the avenue had been leaking – the trees had been killed by the hidden poison which had seeped up through the roots. There are so many lives like those trees, lives that seem to have everything going for them – plenty of friends, good jobs, holidays. Then suddenly, for no apparent reason, everything goes wrong. Somehow insidious, harmful thoughts, spiteful tempers, inflated egos and dark emotions from deep within take over and break up homes and relationships. Lord, help me to realise that I can never take my blessings for granted. I must always be alert so as to keep my heart, my mind and my mouth clean.

You were taught, with regard to your former way of life, to put off your old self, which is being corrupted by its deceitful desires; to be made new in the attitude of your minds, and to put on the new self, created to be like God in true righteousness and holiness.

Ephesians 4:22–24

*   *   *

13th June

The Lord is my shepherd, I shall lack nothing.

Psalm 23:1

This is the seventeenth-century wording: 'The Lord is my shepherd, I shall not want.' Somehow that version has greater meaning for many. The story is told of a little girl who got confused by the different versions when she was learning the twenty-third Psalm and spluttered out, 'The Lord is my shepherd... that's all I want.' What a great privilege it is to be able to approach our God in Jesus Christ with all the unquestioning dependence of a sheep upon its shepherd. Lord, I come to you now in the quietness of this moment... Lead me, enfold me in Your arms... You are my shepherd – and that is truly all I want.

Jesus said: 'I am the good shepherd; I know my sheep and my sheep know me – just as the Father knows me and I know the Father – and I lay down my life for the sheep... My sheep listen to my voice; I know them, and they follow me. I give them eternal life, and they shall never perish; no-one can snatch them out of my hand.

John 10:14, 15, 27

* * *

14th June

Moses said: 'Your eyes have seen all the Lord did in Egypt... with your own eyes you saw those great trials, those miraculous signs and great wonders.

Deuteronomy 29:2–3

Poor Moses! He discovered what every great leader discovers: people *en masse* can be a pain! Moses constantly had to remind the Israelites of their indebtedness to God, of His saving power, of His holy law. Many of them had actually seen that miraculous power for themselves, but their memories were short. We all 'see' things differently from the viewpoint of our own individual situation. Two people see a glass of water on a table. To one it will be half empty, to the other it will be half full. The great poet Blake said, 'The tree which moves some to tears of joy is in the eyes of others only a green thing which stands in the way.' It is the same when people think about Jesus. Some see a well-meaning carpenter, some see a man who tragically wasted his life, yet others see the Saviour of the world.

Open my eyes today, Lord... May the scales of prejudice fall away... Help me to see clearly the trials which others are going through, and to help me to share with them the great wonder of Your love.

*   *   *

15th June

All the animals and all the creatures that move along the ground and all the birds... came out of the ark, one kind after another.

Genesis 8:19

We are becoming far more aware of suffering caused to animals. There is the appalling cruelty inflicted by domestic owners, the suffering caused in the name of research or even for the sake of 'entertainment'. This prayer was recommended by a bishop as suitable for Christians to use when concerned over the plight of animals: 'We pray especially for all that are suffering... for the overworked and underfed, the hunted, lost or hungry; for all in captivity or ill-treated, and for those who must be put to death. For those who deal with animals we ask a heart of compassion, gentle hands and kindly words. Make us all to be true friends to animals and so more worthy followers of our merciful Saviour, Jesus Christ.'

Lord, thank You for the endless hours of joy and companionship which animals give... for the way they make us think of things other than ourselves... and for the realisation that they too are Your creation.

*   *   *

16th June

Large crowds were travelling with Jesus, and turning to them He said:... 'Suppose one of you wants to build a tower. Will he not first sit down and estimate the cost to see if he has enough money to complete it? For if he lays the foundation and is not able to finish it, everyone who sees it will ridicule him saying, "This fellow began to build and was not able to finish."

'Or suppose a king is about to go to war against another king. Will he not first sit down and consider whether he is able with ten thousand men to oppose the one coming against him with twenty thousand? If he is not able, he will send a delegation while the other is still a long way off and ask for terms of peace. In the same way, any of you who does not give up everything he has cannot be my disciple.

'Salt is good, but if it loses its saltiness, how can it be made salty again? It is fit neither for the soil nor the manure heap; it is thrown out.

'He who has ears to hear, let him hear.'

Luke 14:25, 28–35

* * *

17th June

One day Jesus said to His disciples, 'Let's go over to the other side of the lake.' So they go into a boat and set out. As they sailed, he fell asleep.

Luke 8:22–23

'Lord Jesus, you were tired, but were you ever too tired to care? Lord, I am so tired that I can hardly keep going. Give me strength to keep on peacefully so that I do not snap at the people about me who do now know how I am feeling. Give me your kind of strength which in weariness still thinks of others, and when night comes, give me peaceful rest in sleep, and I'll try again tomorrow.' Michael Hollings and Etta Gullick did not mind being honest before the Lord. Unless

114

we realise our limitations, we are unable to ask for help. Lord, being tired is something we all know about – something which You can share with us, I hate bad nights... please help me to relax... to find peace.

> *O may my soul in Christ repose,*
> *And may sweet sleep my eyelids close:*
> *Sleep that may me more vigorous make*
> *To serve my Lord when I awake.*

Thomas Ken

* * *

18th June

All Scripture is God-breathed and is useful for teaching, rebuking, correcting and training in righteousness...

2 Timothy 3:16

> *Tool for employment and compass for travel,*
> *Map in the desert and lamp in the dark;*
> *Teaching, rebuking, correcting and training –*
> *These are the Scriptures and this is their work.*
>
> *History, prophecy, song and commandment,*
> *Gospel and letter and dream from on high;*
> *Written by men borne along by the Spirit –*
> *These are the Scriptures, on them we rely.*
>
> *Gift for God's servants to fit them completely,*
> *Fully equipping to walk in His ways;*
> *Guide to good work and effective believing –*
> *These are the Scriptures: for these we give praise!*

Christopher Idle

Lord, renew in me a hunger and desire to search Your word in the Scriptures. Show me how Jesus was able to base all His replies to His enemies on Scripture. It is not mere history, but Your living word for my life.

* * *

19th June

In His great mercy he has given us new birth into a living hope through the resurrection of Jesus Christ from the dead.

1 Peter 1:3

Mary Austin's little son Mark died of an inoperable brain stem tumour just after his sixth birthday. She wrote a book about the traumatic and harrowing experience of watching her son deteriorate in such a devastating manner, and called it *Living Hope*. At the end of it Mary said: 'We will never forget Mark or fully recover, but with God beside us, we can live again in a new way.' For all those today whose hearts are breaking, whose lives will never be the same again, there is the living hope given to us by the miracle of Christ's power over death. Death is a moving on into a new birth, into everlasting life – a separation of bodies but never a separation of hearts.

> *Though waves and storms go o'er my head,*
> *Though strength, and health, and friends be gone,*
> *Though joys be withered all and dead,*
> *Though every comfort be withdrawn:*
> *On this my steadfast soul relies –*
> *Father, Thy mercy never dies!*

Johann Andreas Rothe

*　　*　　*

20th June

Grace and peace be to you. We always thank God for all of you... We continually remember before our God and Father your work.

1 Thessalonians 1:2

Each day there are millions who travel, and each day crews and staff work to enable the travelling public to get around safely. I once came across this 'Traveller's Prayer' in an airline magazine: 'May it by Thy will, Lord of Heaven and Earth, to take us in peace and safety to our desired destination, there to find life, joy and peace. Guard and watch us who fly the air routes and cross the seaways and travel the overland passes. Make firm the hands of those who guide the steering and sustain their spirits. For in You alone is our shelter, from now to eternity.'

> 'No matter what you may do,' the Lord said,
> 'I shall be faithful and true,' the Lord said,
> 'My love will strengthen you as you go along,
> For you're my travelling, wandering race,
> You're the people of God.'

Estelle White

*   *   *

21st June

Then the Lord spoke to you... He declared to you His covenant, the ten commandments, which He commanded you to follow and then wrote them on two stone tablets.

Deuteronomy 4:12-13

So many people turn their noses up at Christianity and say the whole thing is a series of 'Thou shalt nots'. They can't handle the restriction, so they turn their backs on God. The other day I heard a young mother describe the ten commandments in a refreshing way. She said that when their son began to crawl, she and her husband immediately had to put a gate at the top of the stairs, and they had to say 'No' when he went near the fire or the TV. Suddenly there seemed so many things that he must not touch or put in his mouth – they were saying 'No' all the time. Yet it was only their love for the boy which made them sensitive and protective. They did not have a kill-joy or repressive attitude. Their rules were just boundaries of love intended to keep their child safe. In the same way, she said, God's commandments are boundaries of His love to keep us, His dear children, safe.

How do Thy mercies close me round,
For ever be Thy name adored...
Safe in Thy arms I lay me down,
Thy everlasting arms of love.

Charles Wesley

*   *   *

22nd June

Jesus said: 'If you really knew me, you would know my
Father as well.'

John 14:7

Some people are so regularly on television and in films that
we think we really know them. It is often said that you don't
know somebody unless you live with them – and perhaps not
even then. Many mothers cry in dismay over their truculent
teenagers, saying they don't seem to know them anymore.
Familiarity is not the same as knowledge. The more
communication we have with people, the deeper are the
insights into their characters which we gather.

Lord, today I want to know You. I accept in faith that
through Jesus I can know You. But I don't seem to have
bothered much about communicating with You lately. I've
taken it for grated that You are there, to be called on in times
of crisis. Deep in my heart I know that kind of relationship
with You is no good. I want more than a mere recognition of
You as Creator and Father God – I want to know Your
wonderful peace in my soul.

The Almighty God is with us...
'Be still, and know that I am God'...
The Almighty God is with us.

Lines from Psalm 46

*   *   *

23rd June

Jesus came to a town in Samaria called Sychar, near the plot of ground Jacob had given to his son Joseph. Jacob's well was there, and Jesus, tired as he was from the journey, sat down by the well.

When a Samaritan woman came to draw water, Jesus said to her, 'Will you give me a drink?'

The Samaritan woman said to Him, 'You are a Jew and I am a Samaritan woman. How can you ask me for a drink?' (For Jews do not associate with Samaritans.)

Jesus answered her, 'If you knew the gift of God and who it is that asks you for a drink, you would have asked him and he would have given you living water.'

'Sir,' the woman said, 'you have nothing to draw with and the well is deep. Where can you get this living water? Are you greater than our father Jacob, who gave us the well and drank from it himself, as did also his sons and his flocks and herds?'

John 4:5–12

*   *   *

24th June

Jesus prayed: 'My Father, if it is possible, may this cup be taken from me.'

Matthew 26:39

'But why does God allow extremes of one kind or another to happen to us?' someone asked. The speaker thought for a moment and then replied: 'Yes, it is indeed to test us. It's like squeezing an orange and watching the juice come out. You only know what the quality of the juice inside the orange is like after it's been squeezed'... During the course of our lives we may be called to face an extreme situation. It is only then that all the training and testing of small things truly comes into play. Each apparently small choice was putting diamond into a character that was only carbon before. Each small, good choice, puts such a bias into our lives that in the

119

day of extremity, the day of the big and difficult choice, we will be ready to make the right decision.

Jenny Cooke

Lord, there are so many things I would ask You to take away from me – decisions, disappointments, temptations, thoughts I ought not to have... Help me daily to strengthen my character, according to Your will.

*   *   *

25th June

> Do not be deceived: God cannot be mocked. A man reaps what he sows.
>
> Galatians 6:7

This is a true story. In his early teenage years a boy from a farmstead in Arkansaw harboured a grudge against the neighbouring farm. He tried to think of a way of getting even with the man. One day he hit on the idea of collecting seedheads of the poisonous Johnson grass and sowing the seeds in the farmer's field during the night. When he had done this he felt very satisfied – he had really got one over on the enemy. Years passed and the young man fell in love with a beautiful country girl – the daughter of his neighbour. On their marriage, as the farmer was now getting old, he gave his farm to his beloved daughter and his new son-in-law.

Lord, help me to realise that I cannot do shameful things and get away with it – all my thoughts and actions have repercussions. Be with me in all I say and do today.

> *Sow in our hearts the seeds of thy dear love,*
> *That we may reap contentment, joy and peace...*
>
> W. H. Gill

*   *   *

26th June

For just as the sufferings of Christ flow over into our lives,
so also through Christ our comfort overflows.

2 Corinthians 1:5

The gospel of salvation-wholeness has not eliminated suffering and death. We suffer from time to time, both within ourselves through the sufferings of loved ones and from our sensitivity to the needs of others. But this does not mean that healing is not happening; it lies in the gift of being enabled to see in our suffering the One who suffers with us, and to look beyond death to the One whose promise is that of resurrection life. It is not without significance that the hospice movement which cares for the dying, is one of God's clearest signs of His presence for today's Church and indeed, for today's world.

The Rev. Howard Booth

The more I respond to God's love, the more whole I become, the more sensitive I become, and paradoxically, the more I shall suffer. Any increase in my sensitivity to love, also increases my capacity for being hurt.

Canon Frank Wright

*   *   *

27th June

All these blessings will come upon you and accompany you if you obey the Lord your God.

Deuteronomy 28:2

When I glimpse the limpid light,
What a blessing is the gift of sight!
When birds' song falls upon my ear,
I praise God for the blessing I can hear!

When I walk under spreading trees,
Thank God for blessings such as these:

121

And when my thirsty throat dryly aches,
I know the blessings of seas and lakes!

When in books I've found delight,
I praise God for those who write!
And when I see a soul alone
I praise God for the love in my home!

I am blessed with loved ones far and near
With friendships, interests, talents clear:
My life is guided, loved and free;
My greatest blessing, Christ holds me.

Praise be to the God and Father of our Lord Jesus Christ, who has blessed us in the heavenly realms with every spiritual blessing in Christ... In Christ we have redemption through His blood, the forgiveness of sins, in accordance with the riches of God's grace...

Ephesians 1:3, 7

*   *   *

28th June

'Why do you ask me about what is good?' Jesus replied. 'There is only One who is good.'

Matthew 19:17

The very word 'GOD' suggests care,
kindness... goodness;
And the idea of God is His infinity,
Is infinite care,
Infinite kindness,
Infinite goodness.
We give God the name of Good...

Emile B. Saadeh (Lebanon)

In using the prayer of St Francis I dedicate myself to God's day – to a Good day if I can be a channel of His goodness: 'Lord, make me an instrument of Your peace; where there is hatred, let me sow love; where there is injury, pardon; where there is discord, union; where there is doubt, faith; where there is despair, hope; where there is darkness, light; where there is sadness, joy. Amen.'

* * *

29th June

My God, my God, why have You forsaken me? Why are
You so far from saving me?... O my God, I cry out by
day, but You do not answer...

Psalm 22:1-2

Saint Augustine is credited with saying: 'The best disposition
for praying is that of being desolate, forsaken and stripped of
everything.' That may be true for an ascetic monk, but such
depths of despair leave the average person reeling in secret
agony, bewildered and alone. And yet the glorious truth is
that we are *not* alone, *not* forsaken... Jesus longed to gather
the people of Jerusalem to Himself, but they turned from
Him. He longs to have us turn to him.

Lord, forgive me – forgive my being self-centred and
expecting all things to flow in my direction. Lift me out of
my self-made pit of isolation so that I may see Your arms
waiting to comfort me. I cry out, but if I listen, You will
answer... You are with me.

We have no right to complain of the absence of God, because we are a great deal more
absent than He ever is.

Archbishop Anthony of Sourozh

* * *

30th June

The [Samaritan] woman said to Him, 'Sir, give me this
water so that I won't get thirsty and have to keep coming
here to draw water.'

He told her, 'Go, call your husband and come back.'
'I have no husband,' she replied.

Jesus said to her, 'You are right when you say you have no husband. The fact is, you have had five husbands, and the man you now have is not your husband.'

'Sir,' the woman said, 'I can see that you are a prophet. Our fathers worshipped on this mountain, but you Jews claim that the place where we must worship is in Jerusalem.'

Jesus declared, 'Believe me, woman, a time is coming when you will worship the Father neither on this mountain nor in Jerusalem... Yet a time is coming and has now come when the true worshippers will worship the Father in spirit and truth, for they are the kind of worshippers the Father seeks. God is spirit, and His worshippers must worship in spirit and in truth.'

John 4:13–24

*   *   *

1st July

But You, O Lord, are a compassionate and gracious God, slow to anger, abounding in love and faithfulness.

Psalm 86:15

Jesus is exactly the opposite of all that you are. If you are impure, He is pure. If you are unkind, He is gracious. If you are harsh and critical, He is love. Never spend a moment trying to narrow the gap, but claim Him as the opposite of everything you are by nature... He stands ready to reproduce His life in each one of us.

Alan Redpath

Love is patient, love is kind. It does not envy, it does not boast, it is not proud. It is not rude, it is not self-seeking, it is not easily angered, it keeps no record of wrongs. Love does not delight in evil but rejoices with the truth. It always protects, always trusts, always hopes, always perseveres. Love never fails.

1 Corinthians 13:4–8

*   *   *

2nd July

Jesus said: 'Do not store up for yourselves treasures on earth, where moth and rust destroy, and where thieves break in and steal.'

Matthew 6:19

Why do we hoard things? Because we are sentimental? Because we need security, the feeling of being safe which familiar things give us? It doesn't take many years for our homes to resemble great museums – we have more objects hidden away than in use. When I look around I see all too plainly that material things do not bring happiness. A wonderful home and financial security mean nothing at all if you are going through the agony of depression, or the hell of adultery, or the numbness of bereavement, or the strength-sapping emotional tight-rope of difficult family relationships.

Lord, give me grace to know that my treasure is where my heart is, and I pray with sincerity that You will hold my heart and fill it with a glad response to the treasures of human and divine love – not hidden love, but shared, enriching, indestructible love.

Grant us, O Lord, not to set out hearts on earthly things, but to love things heavenly; and even now, while we are placed among things that are passing away, to cleave to those that shall abide; through Jesus Christ our Lord.

Fifth-century Leonine Sacramentary

* * *

3rd July

Jesus said, 'This is how you should pray: "Our Father in heaven, hallowed be Your name, Your kingdom come, Your will be done on earth as it is in heaven..." '

Matthew 6:9

Christians seek God's will through prayer. Through prayer we will experience close contact with God; and by the power of the Holy Spirit we will be sustained in our sufferings, when facing difficult problems or when we are weakened by the crises in society or by political disagreements. To seek God through prayer is an action that is done not for one's self alone, but Christians must pray for others as well. The Lord's prayer is a perfect plan. Jesus always used the words 'we' or 'our', not 'I' or 'me'. The purpose of our prayer movement is to pray for each other and for those who are deprived of the necessities of life; for those whose rights are denied and those who are being exploited. We must listen with attentive ears and look with open eyes so that we can hear and see and understand, and bring these agonies before God'.

Boonmee Julkinee (Thailand)

Thy will, not mine, be done.

*　　*　　*

4th July

For since death came through a man, the resurrection of the dead comes also through a man. For as in Adam all die, so in Christ will all be made alive.

1 Corinthians 15:21-22

If we ask 'How is Jesus alive today?' 'How do we know He is alive?' 'How can we meet him today?' Do we, indeed, have to refer to an Easter event, a rising of the crucified Jesus from the grave? Or can the experience of Christians today of encountering the living Christ be adequately and satisfactorily translated into the language of 'God's spirit' or 'God the Holy Spirit'?... Can we go further and say that when we speak of meeting Christ today we mean that God who was incarnate in Jesus and made Himself known to the world of men in Jesus still encounters us today as that same God?

Geoffrey Lampe

Christ is alive! His Spirit burns
Through this and every future age,
Till all creation lives and learns
His joy, His justice, love and praise.

Brian Wren

*   *   *

5th July

But grow in the grace and knowledge of our Lord and
Saviour Jesus Christ.

2 Peter 3:18

Lord, teach us to be open to Your Spirit. We want to know
Your will and to do it, but it is difficult to recognise in this
bewildering world. Our occupations and our desires for
ourselves prevent us from being open. Help us to put away
all thoughts and self-preoccupations which hinder the action
of Your Spirit. We so often think that we know what is right
and do not give You a chance to show us what is Your will.
Lord, make us receptive to Your comings to us. Help us to
put away self-deception. that we may grow in wisdom and
love.

Etta Gullick

O Jesus Christ grow Thou in me
And all things else recede...
Fill me with gladness from above,
Hold me by strength divine:
Lord, let the glow of Thy great love
Through my whole being shine.

Johann Caspar Lavater

*   *   *

6th July

'Wake up, O sleeper, rise from the dead, and Christ will
shine on you.' Be very careful, then, how you live...
making the most of every opportunity.

Ephesians 5: 14–15

I've noticed that when the sun shines and when people go off for a drive to the countryside or coast, as soon as they get to their chosen beauty spot they seem to fall asleep! They like it so much and feel so comfortable that they just drop off. Am I in danger of behaving like that in my spiritual life, Lord? When I come to a favourite hymn or song, do I just ignore the words and drift along on the lovely music? In fellowship with my Christian friends, am I alive to their needs or lulled into pleasant apathy, content to be in their company? When Your word is read do I think, 'O yes, I like that bit,' without really hearing it afresh? Lord, You have blessed me with the beauty of fellowship, the beauty of Your creation around me and the beauty of Your holy promises. I must wake up to make the most of every moment. Thank You.

> Lord, as I wake I turn to You,
> Yourself the first thought of my day;
> My King, my God, whose help is sure,
> Yourself the help for which I pray.

Brian Foley

* * *

7th July

What good is it, my brothers, if a man claims to have faith but has no deeds? Can such a faith save him? Suppose a brother or sister is without clothes and daily food. If one of you says to him, 'Go, I wish you well; keep warm and well fed,' but does nothing about his physical needs, what good is it? In the same way, faith by itself, if it is not accompanied by action, is dead.

But someone will say, 'You have faith; I have deeds.'

Show me your faith without deeds, and I will show you my faith by what I do. You believe that there is one God. Good! Even the demons believe that – and shudder.

You foolish man, do you want evidence that faith without deeds is useless? Was not our ancestor Abraham considered righteous for what he did when he offered his son Isaac on the altar? You see that his faith and his actions were working together, and his faith was made

complete by what he did... You see that a person is
justified by what he does and not by faith alone.

James 2:14–24

*   *   *

8th July

And I saw what looked like a sea of glass mixed with
fire...

Revelation 15:2

Sir Isaac Newton was a phenomenal genius. In his so-called
'crucial experiment' the sun's rays were split by a prism into
the colours of the spectrum. Shining one of the coloured
bands through a second prism did not split it any further,
which proved to Newton that white light was a mixture of
'pure' colours. The more we discover about this world the
more it takes our breath away. Newton was, however, a
humble man, and acknowledged his place within the
universe.

Lord, from the people of genius who open up for me
glimpses of Your creation, help me to learn humility, open-
mindedness and renewed wonder.

*I do not know what I may appear to the world, but to myself I seem to have been only
a boy playing on the sea-shore and diverting myself in now and then finding a
smoother pebble whilst the great ocean of truth lay all undiscovered before me.*

Isaac Newton

*   *   *

9th July

From now on all generations shall call me blessed, for the
Mighty One has done great things for me – holy is His
name!

Luke 1:48

After Mary became pregnant she visited Elizabeth and sang

one of the sweetest songs known to literature. In it she makes evident that she has grasped what the angel told her. And what he told her describes as salvation and the remission of sins: here was the news that Mary herself needed a Saviour, and had found Him. The very baby who was encased in her womb would one day offer Himself as a propitiation for her and for all men. And that baby in her womb was God Almighty who had humbled Himself in order to swell among us in the flesh. Indeed, she cries out that God's 'mercy is on them that fear Him from generation to generation'. What is this but the glorious evangel, gospel, that God was in Christ reconciling the world to Himself?

Billy Graham

Great God of wonders!
All Thy ways display the attributes divine...
Who is a pardoning God like Thee?
Or who has grace so rich and free?

Samuel Davies

*   *   *

10th July

How can we thank God enough for you in return for all the joy we have in the presence of our God because of you?

1 Thessalonians 3:9

Thank You, Father, for days, hours or moments of happiness that we enjoy. Our hearts go out in gratitude to You for the beauty of the world, the ecstacy of love, the warmth of friendship, the delight of small children. Thank You for laughter, for music, for pets, for memories, for a new book or a new dress... So many things give us happiness – great things and small – and there are so many kinds of happiness. But we receive it all in thankfulness from You, our Father.

Mary Batchelor

How shall I thank Thee for the grace on me and all mankind bestowed?
O that my every breath were praise – O that my heart were filled with God!

Charles Wesley

*   *   *

11th July

All the believers were together and had everything in
common... Every day they continued to meet together...

Acts 2:44–46

'Together' – one of the loveliest words in the language.
'Together' suggests comfort, understanding, a relationship.
The early disciples needed this way of life – of being together,
binding themselves to each other and helping each other over
difficulties. This was no flash-in-the-pan type of meeting, but
sincere, regular, every-day fellowship.

Lord, I thank You for lives that have interwoven with my
own. I believe You bring us together for Your purpose, even
though I cannot always see or understand those purposes.
Thank You especially for that tender togetherness between
husband and wife – the loving union which is the foretaste of
Your perfect love.

Why hast Thou cast our lot in the same age and place,
And why together brought to see each other's face,
To join with loving sympathy and mix our friendly souls in Thee?
Didst Thou not make us one that we might one remain?
Together travel on and bear each other's pain:
Till all Thy utmost goodness prove and rise renewed in perfect love.

Charles Wesley

*   *   *

12th July

Jesus took Peter, James and John with Him and led them
up a high mountain where they were all alone.

Mark 9:2

Peter, James and John were in for a devastating experience. They would be simultaneously terrified, entranced and exultant, and then, mere moments later, they would have to literally come back down to earth. Sometimes we too catch a vision of something outside time and understanding. We have an experience which is too precious to put into words, and we want to prolong and re-live the moment, to stay with the mountain-top elation. The hymn writer Samuel Greg captured these feelings in his hymn, *'Stay, Master, stay upon this heavenly hill: a little longer let us linger still.'* Samuel Greg was not a cleric but a Victorian mill-owner, a practical man who was very caring about people's needs. He also understood to the need for the human heart to move on with God, to serve Him by serving our brothers and sisters here and now in the dull chores we face. Lord, thank You for the high spots – but make me a faithful disciple in the low times as well.

> *While here we kneel upon the mount of prayer*
> *The plough lies waiting in the furrow there:*
> *Here we sought God that we might know His will,*
> *There we must do it, serve Him, seek Him still.*
>
> *Samuel Greg*

*   *   *

13th July

The Father said: 'Let's have a feast and celebrate. For this son of mine was dead and is alive again; he was lost and is found.'

Luke 15:23

What is it that turns respectable, intelligent children into 'drop-outs'? The parents in one titled family were so embarrassed and disgusted by their son's behaviour that they gave him a monthly allowance of one thousand pounds on the strict understanding that he was to stay away from the family home. The parents could not cope – they were ashamed, and utterly confused and hurt. How thankful I am that my Heavenly Father, however hurt by my behaviour, is always waiting to welcome me. Jesus Christ told His followers that He would never ever turn away any one who turned to Him. I pray for families in which there has been a breakdown of love and understanding. I pray for hearts which are bruised and confused. Lord, give me grace not to judge, and to be always open to reconciliation.

Therefore, if anyone is in Christ, he is a new creation... All this is from God, who reconciled us to Himself through Christ and gave us the ministry of reconciliation: that God was reconciling the world to Himself in Christ, not counting men's sins against them.

2 Corinthians 5:17–18

*   *   *

14th July

King Belshazzar gave a great banquet for a thousand of his nobles and drank wine with them. While Belshazzar was drinking his wine he gave orders to bring in the gold and silver goblets that Nebuchadnezzar his father had taken from the temple in Jerusalem, so that the king and his nobles, his wives and his concubines might drink from them... As they drank the wine, they praised the gods of gold and silver, of bronze, iron, wood and stone.

Suddenly the fingers of a human hand appeared and wrote on the plaster of the wall, near the lampstand in the royal palace. The king watched the hand as it wrote. His face turned pale and he was so frightened that his knees knocked together and his legs gave way.

The king called out for the enchanters, astrologers and diviners to be brought and said to these wise men of Babylon, 'Whoever reads this writing and tells me what it means will be clothed in purple and have a gold chain placed around his neck, and he will be made the third highest ruler in the kingdom.'

Then all the king's wise men came in, but they could not read the writing or tell the king what it meant.

Daniel 5:1–8

*   *   *

15th July

Jesus went up into the hills by himself to pray. When evening came He was there alone...

Matthew 14:23

> *I leave aside my shoes – my ambitions,*
> *Undo my watch – my timetable,*
> *Take off my glasses – my views,*
> *Unclip my pen – my work,*
> *Put down my keys – my security,*
> *To be alone with You, the only true God.*
>
> *After being with You*
> *I take up my shoes to walk in Your ways,*
> *Strap on my watch to live in Your time,*
> *Put on my glasses to look at Your world,*
> *Clip on my pen to write up Your thoughts,*
> *Pick up my keys to open Your doors.*

Anon

Lord, it is only when I am truly alone with You that I can pour out my soul, and fall on my knees, spreading open my heart before You. In faith I draw near in the power of prayer. Receive my prayer, Lord... receive me and strengthen me for my return into Your world.

*   *   *

16th July

Jesus said: 'I am the good shepherd – I know my sheep and my sheep know me...'

John 10:14

The first step in prayer is to know Jesus personally in a one-to-one relationship – the good shepherd, you will recall, called his sheep one by one. The lambs who stay near the shepherd all the time get to know his voice so well that they are able to follow him closely always. The most important factor in any relationship is, quite simply, time. To relate to a person it is essential to spend time with them. Let us respond to this challenge, commiting ourselves to a deeper relationship with God by saying 'I will: I will find time every day to reflect on the word of God, getting to know Jesus better in order to see through Him the reflection of God the Father.

Delia Smith

Lord, open my eyes to realise that people around me need more of my time – my partner, my children, the person I meet in the street who may be feeling so down... Time is caring; time together binds us to one another and to Yourself.

*   *   *

17th July

For by Him all things were created: things in heaven and on earth, visible and invisible, whether thrones or powers or rulers or authorities; all things were created by Him and for Him.

Colossians 1:16

Lord, may I love all Your creation, the whole of it and every grain of sand in it. May I love every leaf, every ray of Your light. May I love the animals: You have given them the rudiments of thought and untroubled joy. Don't let me trouble them or harass them; don't let me deprive them of their happiness. Let me work with Your will and never against it. For I acknowledge that unto You all is like an ocean, all is flowing and blending, and that to withold any measure of love from anything in the universe is to withold love from You.

Adapted from Dostoevsky's *The Brothers Karamazov*

From all that dwell below the skies
Let the Creator's praise arise: Alleluia!
Let the Redeemer's name be sung
Through every land, by every tongue: Alleluia!

Isaac Watts

*   *   *

18th July

Jesus said to Zacchaeus: 'Today, salvation has come to
this house... for the Son of Man came to seek and to save
what was lost.'

Luke 19:9

What an unlikely disciple – despised little man hiding in a
tree! But Jesus chose him. Why am I surprised? Surely it
should be a constant surprise to me that Jesus should want
me – little me, hiding underneath my daily chores and
routines, my outward coat of efficiency and control. Jesus
does not see me as my family and friends see me – He sees
me as I really am. He comes today, to seek me and to save
me, despite every obstacle I push in His way...

Lord, forgive me when I look down on other people, when
I can't see any good in their motives or their lives. Help me
to look objectively at myself and then to humbly offer all that
I am to be used by Jesus, who sees what I can be.

I was lost but Jesus found me,
Found the sheep that went astray.

*   *   *

19th July

But because of His great love for us, God, who is rich in
mercy, made us alive with Christ...

Ephesians 2:4

We look upon parental love as a standard. We recognise its
importance, especially where it is lacking. It is the human
parallel to the love of God our Father. Oh, how we need His
arms about us for reassurance... How I need to find fresh life
and purpose by relaxing into His all-sufficient love... And
right this very minute I do not need to wish or hope or long
any more, for He is here... Thank You, God my Father.

The love of God surrounds us
Like the air we breathe around us –
As near as a heart-beat,
As close as a prayer,
And whenever we need Him
He'll always be there.

Helen Steiner Rice

*　　*　　*

20th July

His mother said to the servants: 'Do whatever he tells
you'... They did so and the master of the banquet tasted
the water that had been turned into wine.

John 2:5, 8

It would have seemed like the social catastrophe to end all
social catastrophes for the wedding feast to run out of wine!
In biblical times hospitality was just about a sacred duty, and
no occasion of rejoicing could be without God's gift of wine.
This story in John's Gospel shows Jesus coming into a
difficult situation and making everyone glad. Dr William
Barclay wrote: 'The trouble about life is that we get bored
and fed up with it... Things get stale, flat and unprofitable.
We get into a state when we can't be bothered and when we
couldn't care less... But when Jesus enters into life, there
comes this new exhilaration, like water turning to wine.'

Now Jesus lived and gave His love
To make our life and loving new:
So celebrate with Him today,
And drink the joy He offers you,
That makes the simple moment shine
And changes water into wine.

Brian A. Wren

*　　*　　*

21st July

The queen, hearing the voices of the king and his nobles, came into the banquet hall. 'O king, live for ever! Call for Daniel, and he will tell you what the writing means.'

So Daniel was brought before the king... [Daniel said:] 'You praised the gods of silver and gold, of bronze, iron, wood and stone, which cannot see or hear or understand. But you did not honour the God who holds in His hand your life and all your ways. Therefore He sent the hand that wrote the inscription.

This is the inscription that was written: MENE, MENE, TEKEL, PARIN. This is what these words mean:

God has numbered the days of your reign and brought it to an end.

You have been weighed on the scales and found wanting. Your kingdom is divided and given to the Medes and the Persians'...

That very night Belshazzar, king of the Babylonians, was slain, and Darius the Mede took over the kingdom.

Daniel 5:10, 11, 13, 23-30

* * *

22nd July

Speaking the truth in love, we will in all things grow up into Him who is the Head, that is, Christ. From Him the whole body... grows and builds itself up into love.

Ephesians 4:15

All praise to our redeeming Lord,
Who joins us by His grace;
And bids us each to each restored
Together seek His face.

He bids us build each other up,
And, gathered into one,
To our high calling's glorious hope
We hand in hand go on.

Even now we think and speak the same
And cordially agree,
Concentred all, through Jesu's name,
In perfect harmony.

And if our fellowship below
In Jesus be so sweet,
What heights of rapture shall we know
When round His throne we meet!

Charles Wesley

Lord, I thank You today for all the friendship I have received... for the good times, the laughter, the sharing and the fellowship of being with like-minded people. Thank You for those who build me up... may we always go on hand-in-hand.

*   *   *

23rd July

Can the Ethiopian change his skin or the leopard its spots?

Jeremiah 13:23

The blind evangelist-singer Marilyn Baker has composed a song entitled '*Jesus, You are changing me...*' It contains beautiful words of obedience and worship. Lord, it is so easy to protest that things can't change, that people can't change, that I can't change, when really all things are possible with You. The sorry truth is that I don't want to change – I'm basically content in my rut, complaining and criticising others, quite happy to count the warts and spots on those around me whilst conveniently blind to my own faults. Why am I scared of facing reality? What have I to lose? Lord, help me and change me. In this quietness I come to You who, being holy and perfect, will never change... With Your constancy and goodness mould a new me.

Faint not nor fear; His arm is near,
He changes not and you are dear:
Only believe, and you shall see
That Christ is all in all thee.

J. S. B. Monsell

*   *   *

24th July

Among the crowds there was widespread whispering about Him. Some said, 'He is a good man.'

John 7:12

The Japanese poet Kagawa wrote: 'I read in a book that a man called Christ went about doing good. It is very disconcerting to me that I am so easily satisfied with just going about!' Forgive me, Lord, that I too fall into the trap of being self-satisfied... I'm going about and I'm very busy, but what have I been doing for You? I'm always going here and there, but am I being with You? I pray for a heart and mind motivated by the love of Jesus Christ and by a desire to do things for others in His name.

> O Holy Spirit, by whose grace
> Our skills abide, our wisdom grows,
> In every healing work disclose
> New paths to probe, new thoughts to trace.
> Grant us your wisest way to go
> In all we think, or speak, or do.

H. C. A. Gaunt

*　　*　　*

25th July

I will lift up my eyes to the hills – where does my help come from? My help comes from the Lord, the Maker of heaven and earth.

Psalm 121:1-2

Where do you turn when in trouble?... Note that the psalmist looked up to the hills because the hills tell us something about God. They have been there a long time – geologists say millions of years. That's a long time! Well, God has 'been there' for longer... There is a stability about hills. They are not here today and gone tomorrow. Neither is God. And so the writer of this Psalm turns from the hills and finds a God who never changes. I want to say this to you – I believe that God has a purpose for our lives, and in His keeping we can come to no harm. So we look to the hills, we press on to the summit – knowing that there is a way through the deep shadows that seem to bar our path at times.

The Rev. John Ashplant

I was pushed back and about to fall, but the Lord helped me. The Lord is my strength and my song; He has become my salvation.

Psalm 118:13–14

*   *   *

26th July

Then I saw a new heaven and a new earth, for the first heaven and the first earth had passed away, and there was no longer any sea.

Revelation 21:1

After many horrendous visions, at the close of the Book of Revelation the author asserts that good will triumph over evil and the reign of Christ will come. In those far-off days mankind will be so brutal and depraved that there will have to be a new beginning. Restoration will not be enough. There will have to be recreation. And so chapter 21 begins, as J. P. Love says, 'Like the quiet beauty of a sunset after a day of storm… But as in such a sunset the splendid colours are generally to be seen climbing over the clouds that still remain, so in John's picture there are glimpses of the angry blackness against which this new radiant light appears all the more glorious.' Lord, forgive all that is past… Create a new heart within me…

The light of God was on its streets
The gates were open wide –
And all who would might enter and no one was denied.
No need of moon or stars by night or sun to rule the day,
It was the new Jerusalem that would not pass away.

*   *   *

27th July

May our Lord Jesus Christ and God our Father, who loved us and by His grace gave us eternal encouragement and good hope, encourage your hearts and strengthen you in every good deed and word.

2 Thessalonians 2:16

Lord, I offer this prayer-poem for those I love who are far away; those who are travelling and all those separated from their families:

Holy Father, in your mercy hear our earnest prayer,
Keep our loved ones, now far distant, in Your care.

Jesus, Saviour, let Your presence be their light and guide;
Keep, O keep them in their weakness at Your side.

When in sorrow, when in danger, when in loneliness,
In Your love look down and comfort their distress.

May the joy of Your salvation be their strength and stay;
May they love and may they praise You day by day.

Isabel S. Stevenson

Lord, I'm so grateful for the miracles of modern communication which make the world a smaller place, which enable us to keep in touch by letter and by telephone. Help us all to feel especially close to You as we hold each other in prayer.

*   *   *

28th July

When they had passed through Amphipolis and Apollonia, they came to Thessalonica, where there was a Jewish synagogue. As his custom was, Paul went into the synagogue, and on three Sabbath days he reasoned with them from the Scriptures, explaining and proving that the Christ had to suffer and rise from the dead. 'This Jesus I am proclaiming to you is the Christ,' he said. Some of the Jews were persuaded and joined Paul and Silas, as did a large number of God-fearing Greeks and not a few prominent women.

But the Jews were jealous; so they rounded up some bad characters from the market-place, formed a mob and started a riot in the city. They rushed to Jason's house in search of Paul and Silas in order to bring them out to the crowd. But when they did not find them, they dragged Jason and some other brothers before the city officials shouting: 'These men who have caused trouble all over the world have now come here...'

Acts 17:1–8

*　　*　　*

29th July

Surely the people are grass. The grass withers and the flowers fall, but the word of our God stands for ever.

Isaiah 40:8

Nothing puts me in my place more than walking on the open moor, gazing at nature as she has been for thousands of years. The span of a human life compared with the full extent of history and prehistory seems as inconsequential as grass beside a granite boulder. I remember the words of an old fisherman – 'You're here today and gone today!' Lord, my soul feels naked and vulnerable – nothing seems to last... and I need someone to hold on to... I need to find some granite bedrock for living. As my anxieties begin to pile up, give me the ability to put my life into perspective... I am only one, and every one of Your children has his or her own need to be met or emptiness to be filled. Fill me, Lord, with the certainty that Your Living Word never changes, that You are with me today and in eternity.

Thy truth unchanged hath ever stood,
Thou savest those that on Thee call;

To them that seek Thee Thou art good,
To them that find Thee – all in all.
                    Bernard of Clairvaux (12th century)

*   *   *

30th July

Crispus, the synagogue ruler, and his entire household believed in the Lord, and many of the Corinthians who heard Paul believed and were baptised.

                    Acts 18:8

I believe in a world meant for everyone to live together happily in.
I believe in living a life of love, sharing and making friends.
I believe this is the way of Jesus,
Who makes me see my faults and my sin,
Forgives me and helps me to let Him make me pure.
I believe He died for me and rose again for me,
And for the whole world,
And He calls me to join the people who follow Him now.
I believe He can use even me
To carry on His work in the world.
So I give myself to Him.

                    John Hastings (A Creed for the Young)

Lord God, loving heavenly Father, I pray today for Your children everywhere. May we all find that there is a special place in which we are to serve You. As Your child, I give myself anew into Your everlasting arms of love and forgiveness.

*   *   *

31st July

When Jacob awoke from his sleep, he thought, 'Surely the Lord is in this place, and I was not aware of it.'

                    Genesis 28:16

144

O Lord, how often have I felt like Jacob? Suddenly I realise how blind I have been, how slow in opening my heart. All the time You have been present. Your glory streams from the dawn sky, Your perfection radiates from every petal of a myriad flowers, Your creative love, expressed through the goodness of my loved ones, surrounds me. We are all so different, yet we all long for the assurance of Your presence with us in our need and weakness. Forgive me, Lord, that I have not remembered you often enough. In that respect I have been a poor witness for my Saviour.

> *Spirit of faith, come down,*
> *Reveal the things of God;*
> *And make to us the Godhead known,*
> *And witness with the blood.*

Charles Wesley

*   *   *

1st August

Lot looked up and saw that the whole plain of the Jordan was well watered... like the land of Egypt.

Genesis 13:10

In this age of technological advance it is easy for us to become dismissive of the achievements of the ancient world. The irrigation systems in Egypt were brilliant, and the nomadic Hebrew tribesmen were quick to appreciate their benefits. Lord, I pray that in this 'nomadic' season of holidays, each one of us will be aware of the lifestyles, customs and achievements of other lands. The more I see, the more I realise how very much I have to learn – I need to accept people more lovingly, I need to see a point of view other than my own. Rush and bustle is not always an enviable lifestyle. I can learn from unhurried days that life is more than work and play. There must be room to stop and water the soul...

> *In this broad land of wealth unknown*
> *Where springs of life arise,*

Seeds of immortal bliss are sown
And hidden glory lies.

Isaac Watts

*　　*　　*

2nd August

One thing I ask of the Lord, this is what I seek: that I may
dwell in the house of the Lord... to gaze upon the beauty
of the Lord and to seek Him in His temple.

Psalm 27:4

Now let us see Thy beauty, Lord,
As we have seen before;
And by Thy beauty quicken us
To love Thee and adore.

'Tis easy when with simple mind
Thy loveliness we see,
To consecrate ourselves afresh
To duty and to Thee.

So now we come to ask again
What Thou hast often given,
The vision of that loveliness
Which is the life of heaven.

Benjamin Waugh

Thou takest the pen – and the lines dance: Thou takest the
flute – and the notes shimmer: Thou takest the brush – and
the colours sing. So all things have meaning and beauty in
the space beyond time where Thou art. How then can I hold
anything back from Thee?

Dag Hammarskjold (Sweden)

*　　*　　*

3rd August

After the wind there was an earthquake, but the Lord was
not in the earthquake. After the earthquake came a fire,

146

but the Lord was not in the fire. After the fire came a still
small voice...

1 Kings 19:11–12

Professor Frances Young wrote: 'One of the things that has
stuck with me from reading that book, *Christians in Ulster
1961–1981* is the emphasis on the importance of the churches
maintaining business as usual in the midst of everything – far
more important that panaceas, slick solutions, escapism or
drastic attempts to produce revolution. When people say
they want to hear a Gospel relevant to this or that situation,
they are perhaps craving the earthquake and the fire, but all
they get is the still small voice. "Pick yourself up," it says.
'Here is the sustenance you need – a broken body and spilled
blood. Go and serve... But lo, I am with you to the end of the
age." '

> *Breathe through the heats of our desire,*
> *Thy coolness and Thy balm;*
> *Let sense be dumb, let flesh retire,*
> *Speak through the earthquake, wind and fire,*
> *O still small voice of calm.*

John Greenleaf Whittier

*   *   *

4th August

Christ is the image of the invisible God, the firstborn over
all creation. For by Him all things were created: things in
heaven and on earth, visible and invisible, whether
thrones or powers or rulers or authorities; all things were
created by Him and for Him. He is before all things, and
in Him all things hold together.

And He is the head of the body, the church; He is the
beginning and the firstborn from among the dead, so that
in everything He might have the supremacy. For God
was pleased to have all His fulness dwell in Him, and
through Him to reconcile to Himself all things, whether
things on earth or things in heaven, by making peace
through His blood, shed on the cross.

Once you were alienated from God and were enemies

147

in your minds because of your evil behaviour. But now He has reconciled you by Christ's physical body through death to present you holy in His sight, without blemish and free from accusation – if you continue in your faith, established and firm, not moved from the hope held out in the gospel.

Colossians 1:15–23

*　　*　　*

5th August

All the believers were one in heart and mind. No-one claimed that any of his possessions was his own, but they shared everything they had.

Acts 4:32

My husband used to joke, 'What's yours is mine and what's mine's my own!' If we are honest with ourselves we will admit that sharing is not easy. But the Christian cannot limit his sharing. Charles Wesley wrote the lines, 'For all, for all my Saviour died.' O Lord, help me to find the unfettered enthusiasm which shone through the early Christians. Help me to realise that all I have is a gift from You, all I am belongs to You. In my life may I acquire the blessed habit of sharing my gifts, my time, my patience and my love with others. It will not be easy – the Book of Acts does not duck the problems and difficulties – but in Your strength, Lord, I face anew my responsibilites as a member of Your family.

> *O use me Lord, use even me,*
> *Just as you will, and when and where,*
> *Until Your blessed face I see,*
> *Your rest, Your joy, Your glory share.*

Frances R. Havergal

*　　*　　*

6th August

The Lord God took the man and put him in the Garden of
Eden to work it and take care of it.

Genesis 2:15

The idyll of Genesis chapter 2 turns sour by chapter 6 when,
because of sin, the world is flooded. It was a global disaster.
Geoffrey Ainger remarks that this disaster occurs 'as a
consequence of human behaviour. So today the 'natural
disasters' that threaten us with extinction are things like
nuclear wars, mass famine, population explosion, the
exploitative destruction of our natural environment. It is
increasingly true of our world that famines, the destruction of
forests and the growth of deserts are not simply 'natural'
disasters. They are also political events, the results of human
choices and human behaviour.'

Lord, I praise You for this wonderful world... Give me a
greater appreciation of its beauty and fascination... Give me
a deeper desire to take care of it...

He reminds us every sunrise that the world is ours on lease:
For the sake of life tomorrow may our love for it increase;
May all races live together, share its riches, be at peace:
May the living God be praised!

F. Pratt Green

*   *   *

7th August

Jesus prayed: 'I pray also for those who will believe in me
through their message, that all of them may be one,
Father, just as You are in me and I am in You.'

John 17:20

Join our hands with Yours and come between our lives,
And join our hearts in love as we meet with You.
Jesus make us one,
By the strength of Your hand accomplish everything You say.

149

And as we live in Your way and travel step by step,
We stand secure in Your life,
We feel secure in Your love.

And in our future lives may we share Your joy,
And breathe the life that You give
Until we see Your face.

Anon

Lord, I praise You for the state of marriage, for the love which enables two people to become one. In the loving and growing of marriage may we glimpse a vision of Your heavenly love, which makes us one with all Your people and one with You.

*   *   *

8th August

The body is a unit, though it is made up of many parts; and though all its parts are many, they form one body. So it is with Christ.

1 Corinthians 12:12

We humans are a funny lot. When we see others whose skin is a different colour to ours or whose cults, rituals, ideas and languages are different to our own, a barrier drops down in our minds. We justify this odd behaviour by taking it for granted that 'different' automatically means 'inferior'. Yet with only one exception, every person born enters and leaves this world in the same way. But through the life and death of that one supreme exception – Jesus, the Son of the living God – we can indeed reach out beyond our barriers to embrace all our brothers and sisters. Yes, we are so different, but we all have need of God and of each other. Christ is our means of global unity, and our means of personal unity. Christ is the beginning of truly learning how to live.

We need each other. Although some of us may be experiencing wonderful times when everything in life is great, other brothers and sisters may not be doing as well. They need our help and support. That's what the body of Christ is for.

Luis Palau

*   *   *

9th August

There Jesus was transfigured before them. His face shone like the sun and His clothes became as white as the light.

Matthew 17:2

On the slopes of Mount Hermon Jesus looked at the darkened sky. Then, suddenly serenity became radiance. From the eternal world there was light, a brilliance, a glory – it shone in His eyes. It glowed in His face. Even His clothes were luminous. He was transfigured before them. Now, at the foot of Mount Hermon there was a problem. A human problem. The inability of the disciples adequately to meet human need. Human nature is always a problem: Paul knew it and for that reason he called for its transformation. Paul pleaded for its transfiguration so that human nature may glow with heavenly light and purity. But how are people like ourselves to be different from what we are?... The first step is to turn to God. We must start by asking, 'What does God expect of me? What is the will of God for my life?'

The Rev. Reg Walker

Do not conform any longer to the pattern of this world, but be transformed by the renewing of your mind. Then you will be able to test and approve what God's will is – His good, pleasing and perfect will.

Romans 12:2

*   *   *

10th August

Jesus said: 'I am the way and the truth and the life. No-one comes to the Father except through me.'

John 14:6

Christ be my leader by night as by day;
Safe through the darkness, for He is the way.
Gladly I follow, my future His care,
Darkness is daylight when Jesus is there.

Christ be my teacher in age as in youth,
Drifting or doubting, for He is the truth.
Grant me to trust Him, though shifting as sand,
Doubt cannot daunt me; in Jesus I stand.

Christ be my Saviour in calm as in strife;
Death cannot hold me, for He is the life.
Nor darkness nor doubting nor sin and its stain
Can touch my salvation; with Jesus I reign.

Timothy Dudley-Smith

Lord, I hold out my hand, I hold out my life to receive Your guidance... Lead me in the way of peace, justice and everlasting love.

*　　*　　*

11th August

But, dear friends, remember what the apostles of our Lord Jesus Christ foretold. They said to you, 'In the last times there will be scoffers who will follow their own ungodly desires.' These are the men who divide you, who follow mere natural instincts and do not have the Spirit.

But you, dear friends, build yourselves up in your most holy faith and pray in the Holy Spirit. Keep yourselves in God's love as you wait for the mercy of our Lord Jesus Christ to bring you to eternal life. Be merciful to those who doubt; snatch others from the fire and save them; to others show mercy, mixed with fear – hating even the clothing stained by corrupt flesh.

To Him who is able to keep you from falling and to present you before his glorious presence without fault and with great joy – to the only God our Saviour be glory, majesty, power and authority, through Jesus Christ our Lord, before all ages, now and for evermore! Amen.

Jude 17–24

*　　*　　*

12th August

Jesus said: 'Again, the kingdom of heaven is like a merchant looking for fine pearls. When he found one of great value, he went away and sold everything he had and bought it.'

Matthew 13:46

I'm told that for a pearl to form a little bit of grit has to get inside the oyster shell. If the oyster cannot get the grit into one place, under control, it may very well rot and die. Out of the poor oyster's discomfort comes a thing of beauty and value; and, perversely, the bigger the grit and irritation, the bigger the pearl which forms around it to protect the tenderness of the oyster.

I'd like to try Lord, to look at my problems and irritations as bits of life's 'grit'. Help me to enfold them with prayer so that they remain under control and in their right place. I pray that out of my pain and discomfort You will bring joy and serenity – qualities of great worth. And may the kingdom of heaven surround me.

Jesu, priceless treasure,
Source of purest pleasure,
Truest friend to me.

Johann Franck

* * *

13th August

Jesus called in a loud voice, 'Lazarus, come out!' The dead man came out, his hands and feet wrapped with strips of linen and a cloth around his face.

John 11:43

The raising of Lazarus has been described as the standard miracle of the New Testament. Jesus meets human need at source and raises each person to wholeness. In Jesus Christ we find *shalom* (peace) for our hearts and minds. This new life is not physical in its origin, but because it revives the spirit within us, our bodies can respond to it. Lord, I know I am guilty of asking for a miracle to suit myself, a miracle that I think should take place. Give me grace to accept that You work the miracle which is needed; it doesn't matter that I don't understand why it is needed. You are in control – You understand – You care – and You restore according to Your will. My Lord and my God, I will trust You.

Expect great things from God: attempt great things for God.

William Carey

* * *

14th August

> Your faith is growing more and more, and the love every
> one of you has for each other is increasing.
>
> 2 Thessalonians 1:3

What a wonderful experience it must have been for Paul, Silas and Timothy to watch other people coming to know the Lord Jesus Christ as their God, to witness growing faith. So often faith is stunted – it becomes routine, almost ordinary. Lord, help me to understand that nothing which is alive remains static – plants grow, children grow, and so too faith must grow, or else die. I ask myself, Have I tried to grow in faith? Have I bothered to care for people in the way Jesus cared? Have I even thought that faith can wait a bit, believing in God's perfect timing? Lord, I pray that You will give me the experience, the will and the patience to grow ever closer to You by Your Holy Spirit.

> *Inspire the living faith...*
> *The faith that conquers all,*
> *And saves those who on Jesus call*
> *And perfects them in love.*
>
> *adapted from Charles Wesley*

* * *

15th August

All sin is disease. It takes many forms. Some of us seem liable
to intermittent fevers; some to self-poisoning by pride and
self-love... We can't produce the right anti-toxin ourselves.
He must enter our lives with His spirit of humility and
renunciation and cleanse us of infection; must blend His
spirit with our spirit to give us of His health. So, too, He
heals our jangled and distracted minds, our turbulent desires
and conflicts, by the infusion of His peace: all the scratches
life has made on our souls. that general sensation of soreness
and stiffness and uneasiness which reduces our natural power
of adjustment to live, the terrible spiritual insomnia in which
we toss and find no rest... somehow – He gives us release.

Evelyn Underhill

*Christ establishes us in God by making us think on such things as cause inward peace
of soul.*

Thomas à Kempis

* * *

16th August

A friend was going into hospital for an operation. I resisted
the temptation to say, 'Don't worry,' because that can seem
very patronising coming from somebody who is one hundred
per cent fit. Instead I felt led to send her a little card with
some words by Mother Julian of Norwich: 'All shall be well,

and all shall be well, and all manner of thing shall be well:'
Repetitive perhaps, but quietly reassuring. The card was
there to greet my friend when she arrived in the ward. It
spoke to us both of our vulnerability and our need for trust in
God.

Lord, I pray for all those who today are facing a worrying
time... May they know, deep within their spirits, that
because they are with You, all will be well.

> *For me, be it Christ, be it Christ hence to live!*
> *If Jordan above me shall roll,*
> *No pang shall be mine, for in death as in life*
> *Thou wilt whisper Thy peace to my soul:*
> *It is well, it is well with my soul.*
>
> H. G. Spafford

* * *

17th August

> But whenever anyone turns to the Lord, the veil is taken
> away. Now the Lord is the Spirit, and where the Spirit of
> the Lord is, there is freedom.
>
> 2 Corinthians 3:16

Lord, I believe that it is only by Your Spirit that I can
understand the meaning of the Scriptures. I pray today for
the veil to be taken from my eyes so that I may draw closer to
You and know that inner security. Lord, I need to be
inspired. You know the thoughts that gnaw away at me
during the day, You know how veiled and clouded my
spiritual vision becomes. I feel confined when I should be
free. I feel dull and heavy when I should be lifted up with joy.
Forgive me that I look to myself instead of to Jesus – that is
my mistake. I look to You, Lord, for this day, for tomorrow
and for all my life.

> *The faith by which ye see Him,*
> *The hope in which ye hear,*
> *The love through which all troubles*
> *To Him alone will turn...*
>
> John Mason Neale

* * *

18th August

This is what the Lord says to the house of Israel:

Seek me and live...
Seek the Lord and live...
You who turn justice into bitterness
and cast righteousness to the ground...
you hate the one who reproves in court
and despises him who tells the truth.
You trample on the poor
and force him to give you corn.
Therefore, though you have built stone
mansions,
you will not live in them;
though you have planted lush vineyards,
you will not drink their wine.
For I know how many are your offences,
and how great your sins...
Seek good, not evil, that you may live.
Then the Lord God Almighty will be with you,
just as you say he is.
Hate evil, love good;
maintain justice in the courts.

Amos 5:4, 6-7, 10-12, 14-15

*　　*　　*

19th August

You are a chosen people... a people belonging to God,
that you may declare the praises of Him who called you
out of darkness into His wonderful light.

1 Peter 2:9

'Chosen, called and faithful,' goes the hymn, 'In the service
royal let us not grow cold.' Singing a rousing hymn in church
is one thing, but how swift are we to praise God in the
hearing of those who don't know him? Embarassment tells us
to be quiet – yet how can we possibly remain quiet when we
have such a wonderful Lord and Saviour? Well, I don't think

we always need to speak with our mouths – often a far greater impact can be made by the way we live our lives. Lord, You have chosen me, You have called me to the knowledge of Jesus, who is the radiance of my day. Help me to feel You in all I do and say, so that others will want to know Jesus too.

Evangelism is to be stereophonic. God speaks to His erring creatures through two channels: the written word (the Bible) and you. The best argument for Christianity is Christians – their joy, their love, their care and concern.

Selwyn Hughes

*   *   *

20th August

O Lord, our Lord, how majestic is Your name in all the earth!... What is man that You are mindful of him?

Psalm 8:1, 4

The Book of Psalms is really the hymn book of the Old Testament. Why is it that verses written and collected hundreds of years before Jesus Christ so capture our hearts and imaginations? For me, the Psalms encapsulate all the basic emotions of human nature. They deal with anger, envy, depression, bewilderment, repentance and love, and in many different ways they open up a vision of the nature of God. The worship of the Psalms is God-centred and not self-centred, and yet they meet our 'selves' totally, just where we are. The Psalms remind us that God meets us when we are at rock-bottom, as well as when we are full of praise and thanksgiving – He hears the tortured cry, 'Why?' The Lord and God of all creation is our Rock, our Shepherd, and our Helper, in any time of trouble. Lord, I look to the Psalms, as Jesus Himself must have done.

Praise be to the Lord, the God of Israel
from everlasting to everlasting.
Let all the people say 'Amen!'
Praise the Lord.

Psalm 146:48

*   *   *

21st August

The Lord declares: 'Set up road signs; put up guideposts.
Take note of the highway, the road that you take.'

Jeremiah 31:21

The prophet Jeremiah uses the idea of road signs to teach a
spiritual lesson. The wayward, pilgrim Israelites were for
ever taking the turnings which led away from God. The
prophets were exasperated. God had given them the Law to
guide them – why couldn't they follow it? Lord, I am a
pilgrim... I need Your guidance, I need to follow in the
footsteps of my Lord, who trod the highways before me.

> *'Don't get too set in your ways,' the Lord said;*
> *'Each step is only a phase,' the Lord said.*
> *'I'll go before you and I shall be a sign to guide my travelling,*
> *wandering race; you're the people of God.'*

Estelle White

*   *   *

22nd August

Jesus said: 'No-one can serve two masters... You cannot
serve both God and money.'

Matthew 6:24

If we want to wriggle out of having to do something we may
well say, 'Ooh, I can't.' Most of the time our 'cannots' are
mere excuses – we can, but we are not going to! But there are
occasions when we use the word because it is literally true
that something is beyond our capabilities. 'You cannot drive
up a one-way street,' says the Highway Code – well, it is
possible, but unlawful. On the other hand, 'I cannot perform
a double backward somersault from the high diving board' is
literally true – such a feat is well beyond the capabilities of
most of us! In the verse quoted above Jesus is trying to
impress upon his listeners the fact that it is beyond their

capabilities to juggle God and their material possessions. We must choose our priorities correctly. Otherwise we will be swallowed up by our desires and ambitions.

> *All to Jesus I surrender, humbly at His feet I bow:*
> *Wordly pleasures all forsaken, take me Jesus, take me now.*
> *All to Jesus I surrender, Lord, I give myself to Thee,*
> *Fill me with Thy love and power, let Thy blessing fall on me.*
> *J. W. Van Deventer*

*   *   *

23rd August

The pomegranate, the palm and the apple tree – all the trees of the field are dried up. Surely the joy of the people is withered away.

Joel 1:12

We more usually associate apples with Eve, the Garden of Eden and – the Fall! The Garden of Eden story warns us that eating the apple of knowledge is always as much a fall as it is a rise. Bishop Richard Harries has this to say: 'In the 19th century most people were taken in by the myth of progress, the idea that life was getting better and better. In our time, the opposite danger is present: the fear that things, are getting worse and worse... So the Christian church has always insisted that nothing that happens, can happen outside God's providence. However far we "fall", we cannot fall outside His care. Moreover, within that providence He is always working to bring some new good out of each new evil.'

Forgive us, Lord, when we are disillusioned by what we hear about and see happening – despite human abuse and misuse, this is such a wonderful world. Help me to see the good in each day and the good in each person, so that my joy in life will never wither away.

*   *   *

160

24th August

May God Himself, the God of peace, sanctify you through and through.

1 Thessalonians 5:23

> *Like the hills serene and even,*
> *Like the coursing clouds of heaven,*
> *Like the heart that's been forgiven,*
>   *Is the perfect peace of God...*
>
> *Like the summer breezes playing,*
> *Like the tall trees softly swaying,*
> *Like the lips of silent praying*
>   *Is the perfect peace of God...*
>
> *Like the morning sun ascended,*
> *Like the scents of evening blended,*
> *Like a friendship never ended*
>   *Is the perfect peace of God...*
>
> *Like the azure ocean swelling,*
> *Like the jewel all-excelling,*
> *Far beyond our human telling*
>   *Is the perfect peace of God.*

Michael Perry

Lord God, grant that I may know Your peace right now.

* * *

25th August

Early in the morning, Jesus stood on the shore, but the disciples did not realise that it was Jesus.

He called out to them, 'Friends, haven't you any fish?'

'No,' they answered.

He said, 'Throw your net on the right side of the boat and you will find some.' When they did, they were unable to haul the net in because of the large number of fish.

Then the disciple whom Jesus loved said to Peter, 'It is

161

the Lord.' As soon as Simon Peter heard him say, 'It is the Lord,' he wrapped his outer garment around him and jumped into the water. The other disciples followed in the boat, towing the net full of fish, for they were not far from shore, about a hundred yards. When they landed, they saw a fire of burning coals there with fish on it, and some bread...

Jesus said to them, 'Come and have breakfast.' None of the disciples dared ask Him, 'Who are you?' They knew it was the Lord.

John 21:4–12

*   *   *

26th August

Philip said: 'Lord, show us the Father and that will be enough for us.'

John 14:8

Jesus is for the Christian the supreme example, says Jeffrey Sharp. 'He was the man for others,' wrote Dietrich Bonhoeffer. In other words, Jesus bridges the distance between man and God – He is God's man and man's God. As such He fills the gap between man's need of grace and God's love. Jesus made himself available to fill that gap, and today He calls His disciples to stand in the person-gap to meet the crying needs around them. Men and women today will only turn from their hurts and pain to Jesus when they see Him alive in His people. So many long to see and believe... They are not sure where to look... Lord, help me to point someone in your direction today...

> *Freely, freely you have received;*
> *Freely, freely give.*
> *Go in my name and because you believe,*
> *Others will know that I live.*

Carol Owens

*   *   *

27th August

Anyone who believes in the Son of God has this testimony
in his heart.

1 John 5:10

Here is a prayer from the United Church of Christ in the
Philippines: 'O God, you have called us into your church to
be Your servants in the service of others. Forgive us for
falling short of Your call. We have loved our buildings more
than our brothers and sisiters. We have been more concerned
with budgets than with justice and peace. We have been
more ready to talk about Christ than to live in Christ's image
and act out God's will for the world... Cut through our
evasions, increase our openness, renew our vision. Make us
more nearly what You would have us be, through Jesus
Christ, whose body we are.

*Witnessing is not a spare-time occupation or a once-a-week activity. It must be a
quality of life. You don't go witnessing, you are a witness.*

Dan Greene

*   *   *

28th August

Trust in Him at all times, O people: pour out your hearts
to Him...

Psalm 62:8

Once, when I was praying and was unable to find the right
words, I came across this helpful advice, written by Francois
Fenelon: 'Tell God all that is in your heart, as one unloads
one's heart – it's pleasures and pains – to a dear friend. Tell
Him your troubles that He may comfort you; tell Him your
joys that He may sober them; tell Him your longings that He
may purify them; tell Him of your dislikes that He may help
you conquer them... If you thus pour out all your
weaknesses, needs and troubles there will be no lack of what

163

to say!' And I felt the Lord speaking directly to me... If I bring myself to Him, I shall never exhaust the subject.

The best way to pray is the simple way – do not use big words, do not search for holy words... Sometimes you don't even need words: there can be a rich blessing in silent waiting on the Lord. Pray by emptying yourself, for it is only by becoming empty of ourselves that we can be filled with His Spirit.

*　　*　　*

29th August

As He looked up, Jesus saw the rich putting their gifts into the temple treasury. He also saw a poor widow put in two very small copper coins...

Luke 21:1

The other week representatives from three different charities came to my doorstep, each with a smile and collecting tin. My reaction to the third was to think irritated thoughts like, 'Do they think I've got a bottomless purse?' However, the experience made me stop and think about charities and the need for them. Wonderful work is done by charity workers for the unfortunate and weaker members of our world family. Their presence on our doorsteps reminds us of our responsibility for others. I recall the word of Jesus: 'Feed my lambs.' Lord, show me that money is not the only gift I can give – I can also give the more valuable gifts of time, effort and understanding. Perhaps I will need some kind of charity myself one day.

Take and use each gift we proffer,
All our talents, large and small.
Lord, You know what we can offer
For the greater good of all.

Judith Winn

*　　*　　*

30th August

May the God of hope fill you with all joy and peace as you trust in Him, so that you may overflow with hope by the power of the Holy Spirit.

Romans 15:13

Lord, I live in hope. A lovely word.

Not the cheap cliche... but a deep root that holds me firm in the bedrock of Your love – whatever comes.

I hope for hope, Lord.

The seeds of light sown in the darkness round Your cross germinate and flower and fruit in the fallow fields of my small life.

My hope starts in your death and resurrection... continues in the certainty of Your presence...

For now, I cling to hope's small seedling. Vulnerable.

Not yet full-grown. Measuring each day in the new leaves of little victories, and – help me, Lord – often in small defeats.

But I still cling to hope. And know you walk with me.

Eddie Askew

We rejoice in the hope of the glory of God!

Romans 5:2

*   *   *

31st August

Do not be terrified; do not be discouraged, for the Lord your God will be with you wherever you go.

Joshua 1:9

Today is the anniversary of the death of John Bunyan. His book, *The Pilgrim's Progress* was written as he whiled away years of imprisonment. Few books have made such an impact on people's religious journeying through life. It was written in hardship and born of experience – that's what gives *Pilgrim's Progress* its convincing power. The world of Bunyan was full of poverty, oppression and injustice, but he held on to his faith and travelled daily with the God who would never let him go. Lord, I need encouragement on my journey... I need You.

> *'No matter what you may do,'* the Lord says,
> *'I shall be faithful and true,'* the Lord says:
> *'My love will strengthen you as you go along,*
> *For you're my travelling, wandering race,*
> *You're the people of God.'*

Estelle White

*   *   *

1st September

Praise awaits You, O God, in Zion;
to you our vows will be fulfilled.
O You who hear prayer, to You all men will come...
You care for the land and water it;
You enrich it abundantly.
The streams of God are filled with water
to provide the people with grain,
for so you have ordained it.
You drench its furrows and level its ridges;
You soften it with showers and bless its crops.
You crown the year with Your bounty,
and your carts overflow with abundance.
The grasslands of the desert overflow;
the hills are clothed with gladness.
The meadows are covered with flocks
and the valleys are mantled with grain;
they shout for joy and sing.

Psalm 65:1–2, 9–13

*   *   *

2nd September

A man reaps what he sows...

Galatians 6:7

The imagery of harvest also contains a spiritual message. We can only harvest what we have sown, and if we sow very little our harvest will be small. As members of the church it is our duty to sow the seed given to us, namely the Good News of Christ. Having sown the seed, the crops need to be tended if a poor harvest is to be avoided. By daily prayers, regular worship and reading of the Bible, the seed sown in us, and others, is nourished and a good harvest can thus be achieved. But... how many of us will suffer from crop failure?

David Bradshaw

> Lord, bless the labour we bring to serve You,
> That with our neighbour we may be fed.
> Sowing or tilling, we would work with You...
>
> Albert F. Bayly

*   *   *

3rd September

Jesus said: 'I am the good shepherd... My sheep listen to my voice; I know them, and they follow me.'

John 10:11, 27

An eighteen-year-old lad called Richard wrote to a minister whom he had seen on television. What he said was challenging, honest and, regrettably, pessimistic, but it nevertheless expresses the thoughts of the new generation: 'People of my age need faith for life when we suddenly break through the barriers of adolescence and learn of bombs and suffering and starvation. We realise our little world of teddy bears and dolls wasn't true, and our world comes tumbling down on top of us. We certainly need a faith. This is when we need to be shown the way.'

Lord, awaken me to the challenge of living in such a way as to give young people the encouragement they need to follow Jesus. Let us fling wide the doors of our hearts and our places of worship; let us lift high the cross of the resurrected Christ, who is the Way, the Truth and the Life.

Souls of men, why will ye scatter like a crowd of frightened sheep?
Foolish hearts, why will ye wander from a love so true and deep?
Was there ever kinder Shepherd, half so gentle, half so sweet,
As the Saviour who would have us come and gather round His feet?

Frederick W. Faber

*   *   *

4th September

*Be joyful in hope, patient in affliction, faithful in prayer. Share
with God's people who are in need.*

Romans 12:12

There is so much need right on our doorsteps, and yet
somehow it is so difficult to know just how to react to people
in need. People suffer upheavals such as a child leaving home
for college, a redundancy, retirement, the loss of a partner
through separation, divorce or death, and the desperate
struggle to come to terms with serious illness. There are no
pat answers or easy words of comfort. Each need has to be
met individually.

Lord, help me to make those in need know that You care.
Show them that it is not weakness to lean on others, but a
natural part of living, grieving and building for the future..
Help me to realise how important it is to be available when
people need encouragement... Give me patience in affliction
and faithfulness in pouring out prayers in Your name.

Lord of all hopefulness, Lord of all joy,
Be here at our waking, and give us, we pray
Your bliss in our hearts, Lord, at the break of the day.

Jan Struther

*   *   *

5th September

Some people brought a man to Jesus who was deaf and
could hardly talk, and they begged Him to place His hand
on the man.

Mark 7:32

Because we can't see anything wrong with deaf people, like an artificial leg or a bandaged head, our attitude to them can be cruelly uncaring. We forget how isolated the deaf – children as well as adults – can feel. Lord, there are so many sounds I take for granted – children playing, the cat purring, footsteps and voices of those I love, bird song, and the sound of the seashore... Today I will make sure I am grateful for the sense of hearing.

Dear Lord, my prayer is for those who live in silence... who never hear music, who feel left out of conversations. I pray for the dedicated teachers of the deaf, for the people who are skilled in helping them medically and for those researching new ways of improving the quality of their lives.

*　　*　　*

6th September

Some of the Pharisees in the crowd said to Jesus: "Teacher, rebuke your disciples." "I tell you", He replied, "if they keep quiet the stones will cry out."

Luke 19:39 and 40

The story is told of a couple who had spent an enjoyable day climbing a mountain in Wales. As they began to come down a thick fog descended, and they were afraid to move. Then they noticed stones piled in the pathway, left by previous travellers up and down the mountain. By following the stones, the couple kept safely to the path and all was well. I am reminded of the great company of Christians who have gone before me, whose lives and example remain in life's pathway as a guide and comfort. Lord, teach me how to learn from others, how to build on their experience because the Lord Jesus Christ was their foundation stone.

Spirit of knowledge, lead our feet
In Thine own paths, so safe and sweet,
*　By angel footsteps trod.*
Where Thou our guardian true shall be, Spirit of gentle piety,
*　To keep us close to God.*

Anon

*　　*　　*

7th September

The soldiers stripped Him and put a scarlet robe on Him,
and then wove a crown of thorns and set it on His head.

Matthew 27:28

When Jesus came to Golgotha, they hanged Him on a tree:
They drove great nails through hands and feet
And made a Calvary.
They crowned Him with a crown of thorns,
Red were His wounds and deep,
For those were crude and cruel days
And human flesh was cheap.

When Jesus came to Birmingham they simply passed Him by,
They never hurt a hair of Him, they only let Him die.
For men have grown more tender
And they would not give Him pain;
They only just passed down the street and left Him in the rain.

Still Jesus cried: 'Forgive them for they know not what they do'
And still it rained the wintry rain
That drenched Him through and through.
The crowds went home and left the streets
Without a soul to see,
And Jesus crouched against a wall
And cried for Calvary.

G. A. Studdert-Kennedy

O Lord, if I have caused You pain by my indifference, or my
self-centredness, I ask Your forgiveness. If I have caused
pain to someone I love, quicken me with Your warmth, so
that I will run to them.

* * *

8th September

On another occasion Jesus began to teach by the lake.
The crowd that gathered around Him was so large that
He got into a boat and sat it out on the lake, while all the

170

people were along the shore by the water's edge. He taught them many things by parables, and in His teaching said:

'Listen! A farmer went out to sow his seed. As he was scattering the seed, some fell along the path, and the birds came and ate it up. Some fell on rocky places, where it did not have much soil. It sprang up quickly, because the soil was shallow. But when the sun came up, the plants were scorched, and they withered because they had no root. Other seed fell among thorns, which grew up and choked the plants, so that they did not bear grain. Still other seed fell on good soil. It came up, grew and produced a crop, multiplying thirty, sixty or even a hundred times.'

Then Jesus said, 'He who has ears to hear, let him hear.'

Mark 4:1–9

*   *   *

9th September

There were no needy persons among them. From time to time those who owned land or houses sold them, brought the money from the sales and put it at the apostles' feet, and it was distributed to anyone as he had need.

Acts 4:34–35

It is harvest time, both in the countryside and in my own garden, and yet my feeling of satisfaction is clouded by my knowledge of the hunger and need being experienced by people in other parts of the world. I feel so helpless to do anything about it... Lord, Help me to take encouragement from the story of the small group who got together in 1942 to help some starving children in Greece... such small, almost insignificant beginnings which have grown into a household name – Oxfam. I pray that these thoughts will grow in my heart like seeds, and through Your nurturing will become a mini-miracle of outreach and caring. I pray for the hungry today, for the homeless and the refugees, for the sick and distressed, and I thank You for the daily miracles worked through all relief agencies... to ordinary people serving their sisters and brothers.

171

For He alone, whose blood was shed
Can cure the fever in our blood,
And teach us how to share our bread
And feed the starving multitude.

F. Pratt Green

*   *   *

10th September

Remember how the Lord your God led you all the way in the desert... to humble you and to test you in order to know what was in your heart...

Deuteronomy 8:2

James Edmeston was born in London on 10th September, 1791. Although an architect and surveyor by profession, he spent a great deal of time and energy visiting and working for the children of the London Orphan Asylum. He was a prolific poet too, and he wrote more than two thousand hymns, mostly for children. His most famous hymn, *Lead us Heavenly Father, lead us o'er the world's tempestuous sea* was published when he was thirty, but became a favourite for wedding services after it was chosen for two royal weddings – one of them that of the future Queen Elizabeth (Queen Mother) in 1923.

Lord, today I remember the children of my country and of all lands... their needs are as great as they ever were... they need love, security and faith.

Guard us, guide us, keep us, feed us,
For we have no help but Thee:
Yet possessing every blessing
If our God our Father be.

James Edmeston

*   *   *

11th September

Sing praises to God, sing praises... For God is the King of
all the earth; sing to him a psalm of praise.

Psalm 47:6–7

The Reverend Ernest Dugmore wrote a hymn especially for
the opening of a small industrial exhibition in his parish.
This underlines the fact that God is the Father, source and
creator of everything we are, see or accomplish. During this
day, Lord, I want to praise You for the ordinary things of life
that I too often take for granted.

> *Almighty Father of all things that be,*
> *Our life, our work, we consecrate to Thee,*
> *Whose heavens declare Thy glory from above,*
> *Whose earth below is witness to Thy love.*
>
> *Thou dost the strength to workers' arms impart,*
> *From Thee the skilled musician's subtle art;*
> *The grace of poet's pen or painter's hand*
> *Portrays the loveliness of sea and land.*
>
> *Then grant us, Lord, to spend ourselves in praise,*
> *To serve our Saviour's purpose all our days,*
> *To speak and think and work and live and move*
> *Reflecting Thine own nature, suffering love.*
>
> *Ernest Edward Dugmore*

* * *

12th September

By the rivers of Babylon we sat down and wept... How
can we sing the songs of the Lord in a strange land?

Psalm 137 1,4

The unknown is frightening. The exiled Jews wept and
wailed as they remembered their homeland. How many
refugees are there who are today grieving in a strange land?
How many people are lying in hospital beds, distressed by

the unfamiliar experience of weakness and unable to praise or pray? How many feel uneasy in a new town or a new school or a new job? May these words written by Eddie Askew speak to us in our need and bring us to realise that there is no situation in which our Lord is not with us. It is only our self-pity which clouds our hearts... we need to find Him again...

Estranged. Alien. Each accustomed act, new,
unknown, frightening.
And yet Lord, You are near. I hold on to Your promise,
'For I am with you always.'
I reach out in the dark for reassurance
And we meet. Touch...
I hold on, warming my cold, fearful fingers in the glow of your presence.
And I realise there are no strange lands to You.
Your presence everywhere.
Your presence, home. Thank You.

E. Askew

* * *

13th September

As the mountains surround Jerusalem, so the Lord surrounds His people, both now and for evermore.

Psalm 125:2

The Book of Psalms contains several references to looking up to mountains and hills, and relates this to an experience of God. The writers used such everyday sights to speak of deep spiritual feelings which they could describe in no better way. Mountains still make us think about timelessness; we still use mountains and valleys to describe our emotional states. We look to the solid, unmovable elements of nature in order to catch a vision of God's unchanging care for each and every one of us. Thank You, Lord, for the priceless comfort of knowing that Your love surrounds me and enfolds me with all who call on Your name. Your love lifts and strengthens us and enables us to praise You, to worship You, to adore You, to call You Father – and then to face the day once more.

174

How do Thy mercies close me round!
For ever be Thy name adored...

Me for Thine own Thou lov'st to take
In time and in eternity?
Thou never, never wilt forsake
A helpless soul that trusts in Thee.

Charles Wesley

* * *

14th September

As God's fellow workers we urge you not to receive God's
grace in vain...

2 Corinthians 6:1

Nymphas Edwards from the Bahamas was inspired to write
this prayer:

Bestow, O lord, Thy heavenly grace upon us and upon all who are called
to be fellow workers with You, that by them Christ may be lifted up
in every land and all men and women draw to Him.
In time of loneliness and weariness cheer us;
in disappointment give us patience;
in the press of affairs keep our spirits fresh;
in difficulties and dangers uphold and protect us;
in success keep us humble; in failure strengthen us to persevere.
May we be joyful in Your service: this we pray through Jesus Christ our Lord.

Lord, I am remembering today my fellow workers for the
kingdom of heaven – those caught up with inner-city
problems, helping the homeless, the alcoholics, the mentally
disturbed, those bruised in body and in spirit... I pray for
those who are administering Your love in foreign
surroundings overseas... I pray for myself... Lord, pour out
Your grace.

* * *

15th September

Jesus said: 'There was a rich man who was dressed in purple and fine linen and lived in luxury every day. At his gate was laid a beggar named Lazarus, covered with sores, and longing to eat what fell from the rich man's table. Even the dogs came and licked his sores.

The time came when the beggar died and the angels carried him to Abraham's side. The rich man also died and was buried. In hell, where he was in torment, he looked up and saw Abraham far away, with Lazarus by his side. So he called to him:

'Father Abraham, have pity on me and send Lazarus to dip the tip of his finger in water and cool my tongue, because I am in agony in this fire.'

But Abraham replied, 'Son, remember that in your lifetime you received good things, while Lazarus received bad things, but now he is comforted here and you are in agony...'

Luke 16:19-25

*   *   *

16th September

With great power the apostles continued to testify to the resurrection of the Lord Jesus, and much grace was with them all. There were no needy persons among them.

Acts 4:33

Lord, I feel so ashamed about the hunger and need in the world at this very moment... The harvests we reap are the spoils of selfishness and greed. We have choked the power of Your Spirit, and the world lies in a mess. Lord, I pray for grace, humility and power to live against the materialistic current, to love and serve the needy, as Jesus taught.

But also of need and starvation
We sing with concern and despair –
Of skills that are used for destruction,
Of land that is burnt and laid bare.

176

We cry for the plight of the hungry
While harvests are left on the field,
For orchards neglected and wasting,
For produce from markets withheld.

The song grows in depth and in wideness:
The earth and its people are one.
There can be no thanks without giving,
No words without deeds that are done.

Fred Kaan

*   *   *

17th September

Give us this day our daily bread.

Matthew 6:11

It is estimated that some thirty-one million people died of starvation during 1978. Since that time there have been some marvellous international fund-raising efforts, but still the starving millions die. It should not be… it need not be… it is a terrible sin. Have you noticed that in the prayer Jesus gave his disciples it says, 'Give us this day our daily bread'? It doesn't say, 'Give *me* my daily bread.' Lord, at this season of joyous Harvest Festivals, I pray earnestly for a caring and sharing worldwide family spirit, so that those who have actually want to share with those who have not.

On Thee we cast our care;
We live through Thee, who knowest our every need;
O feed us with Thy grace, `
And give our souls this day the living bread.

John Wesley

*   *   *

18th September

Jesus said: 'Therefore I tell you, whatever you ask for in prayer, believe that you have received it, and it will be yours.'

Mark 11:24

If you know that you are going to have a day of rush and turmoil and irritation, and especially if, having begun, you find your temper going... deliberately go away for a quarter of an hour and try this: when you are alone and quiet say to yourself, 'The Peace of God is mine.' Poise and peace will become yours. So whatever quality you feel you lack, take hold of it with both hands by faith and in quietness. In quietness and confidence shall be your strength. All Christ's qualities are expressions of His love, and you will find His love the greatest, deepest feeling in the world, flooding into your mind and spirit, bathing them, and refreshing them, and healing them, and when the mind is at ease the wearinesses of the flesh will fold their tents like the Arabs and as silently steal away.

Dr Leslie Weatherhead

> *Have faith in God, my heart,*
> *Trust and be unafraid:*
> *God will fulfil in every part*
> *Each promise He has made.*

Bryn Rees

*   *   *

19th September

> They begged Jesus to let them touch even the edge of His cloak, and all who touched Him were healed.

Mark 6:56

Lord, I am so conscious of the lives needing Your healing touch today. The suffering of some people seems to be so cruel and unnecessary... In these quiet moments, I pray for those I know by name... And I pray for myself – I pray urgently, and perhaps desperately, but I know that in all things Your will, not mine, will be done. Lord, I come in simple faith, needing, trusting, believing... waiting to receive...

> *I receive You,*
> *O Spirit of Love, how I need Your healing from above;*
> *I receive You – I receive Your healing from above.*

I can feel You, touching me right now;
Come, reveal Your power on me now;
I can feel You – I can feel Your power on me now.

John Lai

*   *   *

20th September

One of the high priest's servants challenged Peter:
'Didn't I see you with Him in the olive grove?' Again
Peter denied it, and at that moment a cock began to crow.

John 18:27

On my first night in Jerusalem I lay on my bed listening to
the sounds of donkeys braying and cocks crowing. The story
of Peter's denial hit me. I had assumed that Jesus' prediction
was to the effect that after several hours Peter would in the
end deny Jesus by the time the cocks crowed, early in the
morning. But I was now hearing that sound all the time.
Perhaps Jesus in fact meant that Peter would turn his back
on Him almost at the first opportunity – within an hour rather
than after a whole night. And this applies to me too. By my
actions and my words I deny Jesus, I fall at the first
obstacle... What a miserable friend... what a spineless
disciple...

The Lord turned and looked straight at Peter. Then Peter remembered the word the
Lord had spoken to him, 'Before the cock crows today, you will disown me three
times.' And he went outside and wept bitterly.

Luke 22:61–62

*   *   *

21st September

Is anyone happy? Let him sing songs of praise!

James 5:13

How nice it is to hear someone humming a tune, whistling

179

an air or singing as they go through the day. There are too many long faces about. Forgive me, Lord, if at times, I join the brigade of moaners. I have so much to thank You for and to sing about... I'm reminded of a young man I once met on a twelve-hour flight in a Jumbo Jet. He was blind and he was travelling alone. Towards the end of the journey, which I thought must have seemed like eternity to him, since he was unable to watch what was going on, I asked him how he had liked the flight. He gave a radiant smile and said, 'Fantastic!' Shine Your radiance through me, Lord, as I make the positive effort to see the good in all things and in everyone today. May a song of praise always be close to my lips.

> *Happy are they, they that love God,*
> *Whose hearts have Christ confessed:*
> *Glad is the praise, sweet is the song*
> *When they together sing...*

Charles Coffin

*   *   *

22nd September

If anyone teaches false doctrines and does not agree to the sound instruction of our Lord Jesus Christ and to godly teaching, he is conceited and understands nothing. He has an unhealthy interest in controversies and arguments that result in envy, quarrelling, malicious talk, evil suspicions and constant friction between men of corrupt mind, who have been robbed of the truth and who think that godliness is a menas to financial gain.

But godliness with contentment is great gain. For we brought nothing into the world, and we can take nothing out of it. But if we have food and clothing, we will be content with that. People who want to get rich fall into temptation and a trap and into many foolish and harmful desires that plunge men into ruin and destruction. For the love of money is a root of all kinds of evil. Some people, eager for money, have wandered from the faith and pierced themselves with many griefs.

But you... pursue righteousness, godliness, faith, love, endurance and gentleness.

1 Timothy 6:3–11

*   *   *

23rd September

This is what the Sovereign Lord says: 'In repentance and rest is your salvation, in quietness and trust is your strength.'

Isaiah 30:15

Lord, teach me how to stand still. To switch off; to lean on a gate; to sit and look at your beautiful world. Teach me how to leave the phone off, to slacken speed... Teach me, Lord, to stop – to stop fussing, to stop working at it, to stop keeping on bravely, To stop doing it all by myself...

Teach me, Lord, to let others help me. Teach me to delegate, to trust. That which I do, let's face it, is not so important; doing it alone makes me feel important. It also makes me tired and irritable and anxious and fearful of what will happen if I'm off sick. Teach me, Lord, to stop, to look and listen.

David Kossoff

When you don't have enough time to get everything done, stop for a moment and pray.
Michel Quoist

* * *

24th September

He will wipe every tear from their eyes. There will be no more death or mourning or crying or pain, for the old order has passed away.

Revelation 21:4

Today, Lord, I bring to You in prayer all those whose eyes are shedding the tears of frustration, pain or grief. I pray for the distressed parents whose children can neither walk nor talk; for the husbands and wives who watch helplessly as their partners struggle with the effects of accidents or strokes; for the hearts that are torn by bereavement and feel that nothing will ever be the same again. Lord, there are so many situations which bring tears in this life – and this life is all we know. Through Your messengers, through the words and actions of kind and caring people, bring Your comfort into the broken lives I'm thinking about.

> *O joy that seekest me through pain, I cannot close my heart to Thee:*
> *I trace the rainbow through the rain and feel the promise is not vain,*
> *That morn shall tearless be.*
>
> *O cross that liftest up my head, I dare not ask to fly from Thee;*
> *I lay in dust, life's glory dead, and from the ground there blossomed red –*
> *Life that shall endless be.*
>
> *George Matheson*

* * *

25th September

How great are His signs, how mighty His wonders! His kingdom is an eternal kingdom; His dominion endures from generation to generation.

Daniel 4:3

> *O Lord my God, when I in awesome wonder*
> *Consider all the works Thy hand hath made,*
> *I see the stars, I hear the mighty thunder,*
> *Thy power throughout the universe displayed:*
>
> *Then sings my soul, my Saviour God to Thee,*
> *How great Thou art, how great Thou art!*
>
> *When through the woods and forest glades I wander*
> *And hear the birds sweetly in the trees;*
> *When I look down from lofty mountain grandeur*
> *And hear the brook, and feel the gentle breeze:*
>
> *Then sings my soul, my Saviour God to Thee,*
> *How great Thou art, how great Thou art!*
>
> *Stuart K. Hine*

Great and marvellous are Your deeds, Lord God Almighty. Just and true are your ways, King of the ages... For You alone are Holy. All nations will come and worship before You, for Your righteous acts have been revealed.

Revelation 15:3-4

*　　*　　*

26th September

Then the angel showed me the river of the water of life, as clear as crystal, flowing from the throne of God...

Revelation 22:1

One cool and pleasant evening George was walking along the shore of a tidal river. To an amateur naturalist like him it was a perfect spot, with clear markings left in the mud by birds and animals. The sight of those tracks made George think about the water of Life. As we turn to Jesus, all muddied by our sin, the gentle tide of His cleansing love transforms us: we are washed in His sacrificial blood, cleansed and renewed. After the living tide has passed over us, no trace of our sin remains – just as when the tide washes the river bank, all the tracks are blotted out.

Lord, help me first to be honest about the fact that I do have sins to be washed away – I'm not so perfect! When I can face my sin, help me to be sincere in seeking forgiveness... It mustn't be a routine attitude, or an engineered response. Lord, I must be renewed through the water of life.

> *There is a fountain filled with blood*
> *Drawn from Immanuel's veins:*
> *And sinners, plunged beneath that flood,*
> *Lose all their guilty stains.*

William Cowper

*　　*　　*

27th September

Commit to the Lord whatever you do...

Proverbs 16:3

The Reverend Leslie James is a minister is Guyana who takes his ministry very much to the people. He says: 'You can't lock yourself in the narrow confines of the church. You have to reach out. Life is a whole thing... What is important is the amount of encouragement you can give... I ask myself: "How can we help people to come alive?" Enthusiasm spreads and spreads. We need to take every opportunity for evengelism. I have learned where to find people – at the market places, at clinics, at funerals, at weddings – to meet them where they are. One thing that takes away the anxiety of ministry is that you never know what God may be doing through your commitment.'

Lord, I commit my whole self, my life to You... I leave it to You to guide me to where the people are, so that I will be alongside them at the supermarket, at the toddlers's groups, in the park... Never let me lose sight of positive encouragement or friendship.

*   *   *

28th September

Our Redeemer – the Lord Almighty is His name – is the Holy One of Israel.

Isaiah 47:4

There is a Redeemer,
Jesus, God's own Son;
Precious Lamb of God, Messiah, Holy One.

Jesus my Redeemer,
Name above all names...

184

When I stand in glory
I will see his face,
And there I'll serve my King forever in that Holy place.

Thank You, O my Father, for giving us Your Son,
And leaving Your Spirit till the work on earth is done.

Melody Green

Therefore, God exalted Him to the highest place and gave Him the name above every name, that at the name of Jesus every knee should bow, in heaven and on earth and under the earth, and every tongue confess that Jesus is Lord, to the glory of God the Father.

Philippians 2:9–11

Thank You, O my Father!

*　　*　　*

29th September

Jesus said, 'Do not work for food that spoils, but for food that endures to eternal Life, which the Son of Man will give you. On Him God the Father has placed His seal of approval.'

Then they asked Him, 'What must we do to do the works God requires?'

Jesus answered, 'The work of God is this: to believe in the one He has sent.'

So they asked Him, 'What miraculous sign then will you give that we may see it and believe you? What will you do? Our forefathers ate the manna in the desert; as it is written, "He gave them bread from heaven to eat." '

Jesus said to them, 'I tell you the truth, it is not Moses who has given you the bread from heaven, but it is my Father who gives you the true bread from heaven. For the bread of God is He who comes down from heaven and gives life to the world.'

'Sir,' they said, 'from now on give us this bread.'

Then Jesus declared, 'I am the bread of life. He who come to me will never go hungry...'

John 6:27–35

*　　*　　*

30th September

How great are Your works, O Lord, how profound your
thoughts!

Psalm 92:5

A principle you will need to embrace if you are to become
strong when life breaks you by suffering is this – recognise
that because you are finite you will never be able to fully
understand the ways of God... many scriptures make the
point – the Almighty is in charge. If you are in turmoil of fear
trying to figure out the reasons why God does as He does,
then stop. You can't anyway. Feverishly trying to unravel all
the knots can bring you to the edge of a nervous breakdown.
The finite can never plumb the infinite. Face the fact that
God's ways are unsearchable and unfathomable. Then you
will start to live – really live.

Selwyn Hughes

*One of the marks of maturity is the quiet confidence that God is in control... without
the need to understand...*

Charles Swindoll

*   *   *

1st October

Jesus said: 'My sheep listen to my voice; I know them and
they follow me... no-one can snatch them out of my
hand.'

John 10:28

I've just been reading about one of my favourite people,
Joyce Grenfell. She had a few dotty character traits, but she
was also a very warm, positive Christian lady. In the book
Joyce, which she wrote with the help of her friends, she
recounts the time when she had the dreadful experience of
being stuck in a lift. Her companion was terrified, so Joyce
felt she must remain calm for them both. With great
assurance she said, 'Wherever we are, we are always in the
same place!' What true, helpful words those are. Whether we

are in a lift (hopefully not stuck in it!), in the street, up in the air or in hospital, as children of God we can never be outside His love. So wherever we find ourselves today, we will all be in the same place – in His hands.

> *In His arms of love He doth enfold me;*
> *Words of peace His voice divine hath told me:*
> *I am safe – for God Himself doth hold me*
> *In the hollow of His hand.*

E. S. Lorenz

*   *   *

2nd October

You shall not murder. You shall not commit adultery. You shall not steal. You shall not give false testimony against your neighbour.

Exodus 20:12–16

The Ten Commandments aren't fashionable. We prefer to hear the words, 'You can' rather than 'You shall not'! The story is told of a missionary named Carthew who was teaching his congregation the Ten Commandments. After he had said, 'You shall not steal,' the dutiful audience responded by repeating the statement readily enough. But Carthew realised that the message was not getting through, so he extended the sentence: 'You shall not steal bananas.' Now the people started to wake up and listen. Then Carthew added, 'You shall not steal chickens.' Yes, it is very true that often we mildly accept the generalities without grasping the specific point. Loving your neighbour as yourself sounds very nice, but if you take a long, cold look at the people who actually are your neighbours, it becomes a different and much more difficult proposition. Lord, help me step beyond the words and into the reality of your commandments.

> *For Your holy book we thank You;*
> *May its message be our guide;*
> *May we understand its wisdom*
> *And the laws it can provide...*

Ruth Carter

*   *   *

3rd October

Love is patient, love is kind. It does not envy, it does not
boast, it is not proud.

1 Corinthians 13:4

The actress Gemma Craven was speaking on the radio about
love and chose the well-known thirteenth chapter of 1
Corinthians to illustrate her meaning. 'It is,' she said
'sometimes very, very difficult to pinpoint the meaning of
live, and I think that this is the closest thing in a few
sentences. It is the closest one gets to explaining what love
actually is... If you love somebody very, very much (not
necessarily one particular person – lots of people), then the
love you have for them, if it is a really strong love, is as
strong as the love that you have for God; and if you can love
them as much as you love God, then you are onto a good
thing.'

If our love were but more simple
We should take Him at His word;
And our lives would be illumined
By the presence of our Lord.

Frederick W. Faber

*   *   *

4th October

I will send you rain in its season, and the ground will yield
its crops and the trees of the field their fruit...

Leviticus 26:4

For the fruits of His creation,
Thanks be to God;
For His gifts to every nation,
Thanks be to God.
For the ploughing, sowing, reaping,
Silent growth while we are sleeping,
Future needs in earth's safe-keeping,
Thanks be to God.

In the just reward of labour,
             God's will is done.
In the help we give our neighbour,
             God's will is done;
In our world-wide task of caring
For the hungry and despairing,
In the harvests we are sharing
             God's will is done.

                                    Fred Pratt Green

Lord, as I think about the infinitely varied shapes, colours
and tastes of Your creations – the fruits, vegetables, trees and
flowers – my heart is overwhelmed by beauty and gratitude.

*   *   *

5th October

Jesus said: 'Children, how hard it is to enter the kingdom
of God! It is easier for a camel to go through the eye of a
needle than for a rich man to enter the kingdom of God.'

                                    Mark 10:25

Professor William Barclay was a great biblical scholar, and
one who showed the relevance of biblical teaching to our
contemporary world. This is what he had to say about riches:
'It's not wrong to want material things. A man is perfectly
right to want to support himself and his family... but it is
wrong to grow so immersed in the things and the activities of
this world that they become our main interest in life. The
three great dangers of riches are that they encourage a false
independence, and we can never be independent of God;
they fix our thoughts upon this world and make us forget that
there is another world; they tend to make us selfish because it
is human nature to want more than we have.' Lord, save me
from selfishness... all I have is Your gift to me.

All to Jesus I surrender, all to Him I freely give...
All to Jesus I surrender, humbly at His feet I bow,
Worldly pleasures all forsaken, take me Jesus, take me now.
                                    J. W. Van Deventer

*   *   *

6th October

David praised the Lord in the presence of the whole
assembly, saying:

> 'Praise be to You, O Lord,
> God of our father Israel,
> from everlasting to everlasting.
> Yours, O Lord, is the greatness and the power
> and the glory and the majesty and the splendour,
> for everything in heaven and earth is Yours.
> Yours, O Lord, is the kingdom;
> You are exalted as head over all.
> Wealth and honour come from You;
> You are the ruler of all things.
> In Your hands are strength and power
> to exalt and give strength to all.
> Now, our God, we give You thanks,
> And praise Your glorious name.

'But who am I, and who are my people, that we should be
able to give as generously as this? Everything comes from
You, and we have given You only what comes from Your
hand.'

1 Chronicles 29:10–15

*   *   *

7th October

But you, dear friends, build yourselves up in your most
holy faith and pray in the Holy Spirit.

Jude 20

Faith must have content and it must not take us into a
fantasy, fairy-tale world of wishful thinking divorced from
the realities of human experience, whether in our everyday
lives or as the result of scientific discovery... Faith must now
reckon with all races and religions, with many different
cultures, and with the fact that all religions have done evil as
well as good, so that religion as such is not salvation either for

190

individuals or humankind. Yet we are, in St Paul's words, members one of another and ultimately the welfare of each depends upon the welfare of all. But faith must also safeguard the mystery of God and not claim that it can explore the utmost depts of His being or manipulate Him to its own conceived advantage.

G. S. Wakefield

Life, after all, at its deepest is a stretching out of faith and love to God in the dark.
Baron von Hugel

*   *   *

8th October

And the peace of God, which transcends all under-standing, will guard your hearts and your minds in Christ Jesus.

Philippians 4:7

A viewer wrote to Rev John Ashplant after one of his television talks to tell him how, in the midst of the horrors of the First World War, he had come to know the reality of God's peace. A million muddy miles from his home, he had experienced the peace of God within himself. Scientists tell us that deep in the oceans there are waters that remain still through the fiercest of surface storms. How much cooler and more constant my life would be if I had a profound certainty within my heart like the stillness of those deep waters... Lord, I pray for Your peace... for the wholeness and well-being which comes from complete trust in You.

The peace of God is a positive thing. It isn't just the absence of noise, nor is it the absence of problems and difficulties – it is the kind of peace you can know in the midst of a storm... You cannot buy it, you cannot earn it, you cannot learn it. But you can receive it from the Prince of Peace himself.

The Rev. John Ashplant

*   *   *

191

9th October

You are all sons of God through faith in Christ Jesus... If
you belong to Christ, then you are Abraham's seed, and
heirs according to the promise.

Galatians 3:26–29

In any organisation, be it the Brownies or the Women's
Institute, there is a feeling of common pride and loyalty – a
shared enjoyment in belonging to a group, which in its turn
belongs to a greater family. No human being wants to be
isolated – we all need to belong to something or someone. In
the great Christian family we share the joy of belonging to
Jesus Christ. Lord, I can't really grasp what this means...
forgive me that I so often treat belonging to You as just a part
of my social life – I put in an appearance when there is
something going on which specially interests me, and I get
irritated if I'm asked to do something extra. Help me to
understand that belonging means involvement, commitment
and togetherness...

*Get your perspective restored day after day. He is God and you belong to Him.
Everything else is secondary to that wonderful fact. Let it grip you... flood your heart!*
Michael Baughen

* * *

10th October

But while he [the son] was still a long way off, his father
saw him and was filled with compassion for him; he ran to
his son, threw his arms around him and kissed him.

Luke 15:20

This is possibly the most famous of the parables which Jesus
told. The phrase 'prodigal son' has passed into our language,
a prodigal being a wasteful person, and yet also a repentant
and reformed character in the end. In Jesus's story the
younger son had all the benefits of being a son and all the
security of being at home, but he thought it would be far

more exciting to leave home... Within the family of the church people have all the benefits of fellowship, and yet there is the disturbing little voice which whispers that life outside has more to offer. We want to behave differently, with no-one looking over our shoulders – we want to be 'free'. Not till we have lost what we took for granted do we realise just how blessed we were. Lord, my loving Father, if there is need in my life for reconciliation, give me grace to begin that process today.

Working for reconciliation does not mean continually looking back, nor yet standing still. Rather it is a challenge to move forward in faith and hope with a deep and growing love for all humankind, and for the whole creation God has give us.

Uniting Church, Australia

*   *   *

11th October

But thanks be to God! He gives us the victory through our lord Jesus Christ. Therefore, my dear brothers, stand firm.

1 Corinthians 15:57

Lord, forgive me that I so easily feel defeated. Where is my vision, my joy, my thanks? I should have a heart that is bubbling with joy because of the victory which has been secured for me and for all who claim Jesus as Lord. Yes, I will give thanks... I will stand firm... The American writer Os Guinness has written: 'Nothing is more characteristic of Christian faith than its emphatic affirmation of the complete victory of Jesus Christ over the powers of darkness. Biblical doctrine and Christian experience are one. Christ is victor and there is no power in heaven or earth, in the present or future that can stand against Him.'

Thine be the glory, risen conquering Son,
Endless is the victory Thou o'er death hast won.

Edmond L. Budry

*   *   *

12th October

Aim for perfection, listen to my appeal, be of one mind,
live in peace. And the God of Love and peace be with
you.

2 Corinthians 13:11

We pray for peace,
Not the easy peace built on complacency
And not the truth of God;
We pray for real peace –
The peace God's love alone can seal.

We pray for peace,
But not the cruel peace leaving God's poor bereft
And dying in distress;
We pray for real peace –
Enriching all humanity.

We pray for peace,
Holy Communion with our risen Lord
And all humanity;
God's will fulfilled on earth,
And all His creatures reconciled.

Alan Gaunt

May we carry in the chalice of our hearts the blessing of
Love's peace, and distribute it through all the ways of our
going.

Michael Walton

*   *   *

13th October

One of the teachers of the law asked Jesus, 'Of all the
commandments, which is the most important?'
  'The most important one,' answered Jesus, 'is this:
"Hear, O Israel, the Lord our God, the Lord is one.
Love the Lord your God with all your heart and with all
your soul and with all your mind and and with all your
strength." The second is this: "Love your neighbour as

194

yourself.'' There is no commandment greater than these.'

'Well said, teacher,'' the man replied. 'You are right in saying that God is one and there is no other but Him. To love Him with all your heart, with all your understanding and with all your strength, and to love your neighbour as yourself is more important than all burnt offerings and sacrifices.'

When Jesus saw that he had answered wisely, He said to him, 'You are not far from the kingdom of God.' And from then on no-one dared ask Him any more questions.

Mark 12:29–34

*　　*　　*

14th October

Jesus said: 'It is written, ''My house shall be a house of prayer''; but you have made it ''a den of robbers''.'

Luke 19:46

It's a very sad fact, but everywhere people go they seem unerringly bent on twisting the purpose of God. Jesus saw how the holy Temple had been tainted by the money-changers and the traders. They had blotted out prayer by their greed. Today in holy places we still find the human effort to confine God and to serve Him up in bite-sized and profitable pieces. But as the apostle Paul wrote, 'God cannot be mocked.' And God cannot be confined. The house or temple He requires is the obedient and willing heart of the Christian... He is not restricted to marble and stone buildings which cost millions of pounds to maintain... He does not wait for us to make our way to church. He is with us and in us and around us. Lord, forgive me and the world for our foolish ways – I come to You by faith in simple prayer.

Do you not know that your body is a temple of the Holy Spirit, who is in you, whom you have received from God? You are not your own; you were bought at a price. Therefore honour God with your body.

1 Corinthians 6:19–20

*　　*　　*

195

15th October

Jesus said: 'I have come into the world as a light, so that
no-one who believes in me should stay in darkness.'

John 12:46

We need to find God, and he cannot be found in noise and
restlessness. God is the friend of silence. See how nature –
trees, flowers, grass – grows in silence: see how the stars, the
moon and sun, how they move in silence... The more we
receive in silent prayer, the more we can give in our active
life. We need silence to be able to touch souls. The essential
thing is not what we say, but what God says through us. All
our words will be useless unless they come from within –
words which do not give the light of Christ increase the
darkness.

Mother Teresa of Calcutta

*Lord, I just ask for the light of Your love to shine in my little world. In being still and
silent, may I grow in the nurture of Your love so that without any fear I can embrace
those still in darkness. Jesus, be my light.*

*　　*　　*

16th October

'Sir,' the invalid replied [to Jesus], 'I have no-one to help
me into the pool when the water is stirred.'

John 5:7

A few miles from where I live there is a pioneer centre for
physically handicapped people of all ages. Some come on
holiday from special homes, and for most it is the first time
they have been able to get onto a beach or out in a boat.
There is nothing remarkable about the area – the same thing
could be done in many other places on the coast. What is
remarkable, however, is the person-to-person care at the
pioneer centre. Some of the people who arrive there need the
constant care of two able-bodied friends, yet with that special

help there is hardly any activity they do not sample. Oh, the bleak and soul-destroying sigh, 'I have no-one to help me...' The joy and sense of achievement on the faces of the physically handicapped at that centre witness to the miracle of a helping hand. Lord, what have I done for somebody else...?

> *O Christ, the Healer, we have come*
> *To pray for health, to plead for friends.*
> *How can we fail to be restored*
> *When reached by love that never ends?*
>
> *Grant that we all, made one in faith,*
> *In Your community may find*
> *The wholeness that, enriching us,*
> *Shall reach and shall enrich mankind.*

F. Pratt Green

* * *

17th October

> The people said to Joshua... 'We will serve the Lord.'
> Then Joshua said, 'You are witnesses against yourselves
> that you have chosen to serve the Lord.'
>
> Joshua 24:21

Joshua had pinned the Israelites down to making a decision! In a period of sober reflection and repentance, their choice was to serve and obey God. But we all know how much easier it is to say we will do such and such than to put the decision into action. Jeff Sharp puts it like this: 'Nothing is ever achieved until someone somewhere sets their mind to do something. The same is true in the matter of evangelism. Men and women of our age will only turn to Jesus from their hurts and pain when they see Jesus alive in His people. It is as He is able to express His life through His people that our contemporaries will turn from envy, bitterness and selfishness.'

197

Lord crucified – give me a heart like Thine...
Teach me to love the dying souls of men;
And keep my heart in closest touch with Thine.
And give me love –
Pure Calvary love to bring the lost to Thee...

Anon

*   *   *

18th October

Jesus said: 'Others, like seed sown on good soil, hear the
word, hear the word, accept it, and produce a crop –
thirty, sixty, or even a hundred times what was sown.'

Mark 4:20

I once heard the story of a young man who sailed for Canada
to seek his fortune. But, working as a farm-hand, he soon
grew homesick for this native Scotland, and so he returned.
However, he was very fond of the farmer who had employed
and befriended him, and so bought a gift to send out to him
in Canada. Just before the Scotsman sent the gift, he scooped
up a handful of the fine wheat which was being unloaded at
the dockside, and slipped it into the package. The Canadian
farmer sowed the grain – it was ideal for the conditions and
gave a better yield than any other variety. Soon it was being
used throughout the region. It was named 'red Fife' and over
the years millions of bushels of it were produced from that
one handful. Who can tell what God can accomplish if we
give to him the little we have to offer?

Praise God for the harvest of conflict and love,
For leaders and peoples who struggle and serve
To conquer oppression, earth's plenty increase,
And gather God's harvest of justice and peace.

Brian A. Wren

*   *   *

19th October

Jesus said: 'The harvest is plentiful, but the workers are few. Ask the Lord of the harvest, therefore, to send out workers into His harvest field.'

Luke 10:2

There is so much loneliness and heartache on our city streets, and such a need for workers to go alongside those who cannot cope and bring Christ's love to them. Often it seems a thankless, hopeless task, but one young missionary has told the story of a 'victory'. He found a well-educated man living in squalor, and freezing cold rags on a floor. The missionary visited him time after time, assuring the man of the new life that was available to him through faith. He prayed for him and with him. Eventually, the man exchanged his filthy old clothes for clean, tidy ones, shaved and joined the congregation of the local church. The young missionary praised God that the bruised life was wholly transfigured by the Holy Spirit.

Lord, I pray for those who are today without hope. The city streets can be derelict jungles of despair – I am humbled by the love shown by Christians who deny themselves in order to seek and to save in the name of Jesus. May the harvest be plentiful and the workers more numerous.

*   *   *

20th October

While Jesus was walking in the temple courts, the chief priests, the teachers of the law and the elders came to Him. 'By what authority are you doing these things?' they asked. 'And who gave you authority to do this?'

Jesus replied, 'I will ask you one question. Answer me, and I will tell you by what authority I am doing these things. John's baptism – was it from heaven, or from men? Tell me!'

They discussed it among themselves and said, 'If we say, "From heaven," He will ask, "Then why didn't you

199

believe him?'' But if we say, "From men"...' (They feared the people, for everyone held that John really was a prophet).

So they answered Jesus, 'We do not know.'

Jesus said, 'Neither will I tell you by what authority I am doing these things.'

Mark 11:27–33

*　　*　　*

21st October

It was cold, and the servants and officials stood around a fire they had made to keep warm. Peter also was standing with them, warming himself.

John 18:18

Why is it that an open fire is so irresistable? We feel warmer just seeing the fire, long before the warmth has penetrated to our toes. Adverts for open fires use caressing music and shots of fireside pets sprawling contentedly to gain our attention and tempt us to buy. Fire has been called a useful friend but a lethal enemy, and that is true. There is warmth and comfort in a fire's glowing embers, but there is also horrific danger in its leaping flames. Fire is part of life, and the Bible writers often mentioned it when writing about God's activity. The Gospel accounts of the first Easter include three fires. The first is the open-air fire at which Peter comforts himself; the second is the inner fire which the two friends feel as they walk with Jesus on the Emmaus road; and the third is the fire that Jesus has ready for the disciples after their night's fishing.

This Easter do we deny, are we unsure, or do we fully recognise the fire of the love of Christ when it burns within us?

Noelene Martin

*　　*　　*

22nd October

The queen, hearing the voices of the king and his nobles,
came into the banquet hall... 'Call for Daniel, and he will
tell you what the writing means.'

Daniel 5:10-12

King Belshazzar was having a good time – all his noblemen,
wives and concubines were having a rave-up, drinking wine
from the gold and silver goblets which his father had.
plundered from the temple in Jerusalem. Belshazzar was
doing precisely what he pleased, and the party was in full
swing. Suddenly, the ominous writing appeared on the wall –
this was so vivid a happening that the phrase 'writing on the
wall' still lives on after over two and a half thousand years.
Frivolity turned to fear. The king's mother swept into the
hall to tell her son to fetch Daniel. She knew in her heart that
her son was going to lose all that his father had built up, yet
she recognised God's hand to be greater than human power.
Probably, like mothers in every generation, she had warned
her son and had prayed that he would behave differently. In
the end she was there to witness his murder.

*Lord, I pray today for mothers whose children's lives are burdens pressing heavily on
their hearts... mothers whose sons are in prison for violence, cruelty, gambling,
drunkenness, drug addiction, rape or murder... those suffering, anonymous women
who cannot help loving and yet are so hurt. Their love is like Your constant love for
this sinful world.*

*   *   *

23rd October

Jesus said: 'Light has come into the world, but men loved
darkness instead of light because their deeds were evil.'

John 3:19

Light – torchlight, candlelight, sunlight, electric light, search
light, distant light... so many lights. We can be so
conveniently vague about the Light that came into the world;

there are as many interpretations of it as there are people to think about it. Many look on Jesus as a 'Christmas Light', a once-a-year novelty; others acknowledge a light, but it is for them like seeing a car headlight far away – there is no immediate light around them. It is different for those who kneel before Jesus, the Light of the World: the radiance of His holiness warms and illumines their hearts, and shining in, through and around them, tearing away the darkness of their unworthiness... Lord, shine your light and love into my life.

Jesus does not patch things up. He renews. If you will ask Him to go back with you to that dark spot in your life, He will change its darkness into Light.

Corrie ten Boom

* * *

24th October

But who can endure the day of His coming?... for He will
be like a refiner's fire or a launderer's soap.

Malachi 3:2

What an unusual vision – the day of judgement like a launderette! But of course, washing and purifying are basic needs for garments as well as souls. The Bible writers never cut religion out of everyday things. Their God was so real that He was in all things, and every action either confirmed or denied His lordship. Over the centuries the church has mistakenly come to assume that worship is accomplished once or twice on a Sunday, somewhere 'different' – that is, in a consecrated building. We seem to think that we merely 'visit' God like we would an aged relative, out of duty. But the glorious truth is that God is around us, within us, behind us and before us. And that same Father – God is able to cleanse our hearts and minds at the very moment we confess our need.

Lord, I know the advertisements for soap powders off by heart – and here I am struggling to find the right words in order to say that I need washing... washing in the blood of the Lamb. Renew and recreate me as You would have me be.

* * *

25th October

> Jesus said: 'And when you stand praying, if you hold anything against anyone, forgive him, so that your Father in heaven may forgive you your sins.'
>
> Mark 11:25

What does this forgiving love do? It helps us accept one another and things as they are. One of the problems many of us have to face is that of bumping into one another rather like snooker balls on the table. We hit or touch one another and bounce into others, bruising and being bruised. Forgiving love can be like the cork that placed between the snooker balls will absorb the tension and pressure. Jesus in His love placed Himself at the point of human tension and pain, absorbing the shock and taking the hurt... How are we to live this life of love?... As Jesus lived on earth and now lives in the glory of heaven. We are to be forgiving.

Jeffrey Sharp

Jesus, Lamb of God: have mercy upon me.
Jesus, bearer of my sins: have mercy upon me.
Jesus, Redeemer of the world: give me Your peace.

* * *

26th October

> And pray in the Spirit on all occasions with all kinds of prayers and requests. With this in mind, be alert and always keep on praying for all the saints.
>
> Ephesians 6:18

If you are feeling a bit down and prayer isn't coming very easily today, read these words by the late Catherine Bramwell-Booth: 'You have such ups and downs. Some days you feel you can face the world, the flesh and the devil single-handed. And another day you feel you're no good... I've been praying for someone recently that I've been very disappointed in. Whenever I pray for him by name, I'm tempted to feel, 'What's the good of this? What good can my praying do? I don't know. I don't understand. But I do know that Jesus said we ought always to pray and not to faint. Well, there's the choice... either pray and trust or faint and give up the whole thing. I can't contemplate that!'

> *Pray always: pray and never faint; pray without ceasing, pray.*
> *Pour out your souls to God:*
> *Your guides and brethren bear for ever on your mind;*
> *Extend the arms of mighty prayer in grasping all mankind.*
>
> Charles Wesley

*　　*　　*

27th October

As you come to him, the Living Stone – rejected by men but chosen by God and precious to Him – you also, like living stones, are being built into a spiritual house to be a holy priesthood, offering spiritual sacrifices acceptable to God through Jesus Christ. For in Scripture it says:

> *See, I lay a stone in Zion,*
> *a chosen and precious cornerstone,*
> *and the one who trusts in Him*
> *will never be put to shame.*

Now to you who believe, this stone is precious. But to those those who do not believe,

> *The stone the builders rejected*
> *has become the capstone,*

and,

> *A stone that causes men to stumble*
> *and a rock that makes them fall.*

They stumble because they disobey the message... But you are a chosen people... a people belonging to God... that you may declare the praises of Him who called you out of darkness into His wonderful light.

1 Peter 2:4–10

*　　*　　*

28th October

Peter said, 'Lord, You know all things...'

John 21:17

Some days I feel as though I don't know anything anymore. I am perplexed, bewildered and frightened about the world, about those close to me and even about myself. I will take comfort in knowing that other people sometimes feel like this too. Lord, draw near to me as I read the thoughts of Your servant Dietrich Bonhoeffer, and help me in my doubting to believe that You know all things – that You know me and will never leave me.

> *Who am I? This one or the other?*
> *Am I one person today and tomorrow another?*
> *Am I both at once, a hypocrite before others,*
> *And before myself a contemptible, woebegone weakling?*
> *Or is something within me still like a beaten army*
> *Fleeing in disorder from victory already achieved?*
> *Who am I? They mock me, these lonely questions of mine.*
> *Whoever I am, Thou knowest, O God, I am Thine!*

Dietrich Bonhoeffer

*   *   *

29th October

Jesus replied, 'Love the Lord your God with all your heart and with all your soul and with all your mind. This is the first and greatest commandment.'

Matthew 22:37

It has been said that the gods we make are infinitely smaller than the God who made us, and that a god small enough for our understanding would not be large enough for our needs. That is why the workings of God must of necessity always remain a mystery, leaving us mortals to trust God's meaning... You can never be absolutely sure of the road – we are pilgrims stumbling along in the guiding darkness. Most strongly do I believe that there is a God, a loving God, and that in Him we live, move and have our being. I know in faith that this power is at work in my life and therefore in my work too.

Mary O'Hara

This, this is the God we adore,
Our faithful, unchangeable Friend,
Whose love is as great as His power,
And neither knows measure nor end.

Joseph Hart

*   *   *

30th October

Jesus said, 'Suppose one of you has a hundred sheep and loses one of them. Does he not leave the niney-nine and go after the lost sheep until he finds it? And when he finds it, he joyfully puts it on his shoulders and goes home.'

Luke 15:4–5

Have you ever thought what a tender picture this is? The common reaction to a missing sheep, or to one that had intruded where it had no business, would have been to shoo it home with cross words. Mercifully, this is not the way God acts when we have 'gone astray'. He seeks us and rescues in the midst of our terrors, our disorientation, our loneliness and despair... He lifts us out of the pits we have dug for ourselves; but more than this, He does not leave us alone to find our own way back – He carries us.

Dear Lord, I'm old enough and big enough to walk on my own, but I long to be carried – to feel taken back into the joyful companionship and safety of Your presence. Forgive me for wandering... I did not realise I had gone so far. Thank You for rescuing me – for bloodying Your hands for my sake... Thank you.

Perverse and foolish oft I strayed,
But yet, in love, He sought me;
And on His shoulder gently laid
And home rejoicing brought me.

Henry W. Baker

*   *   *

31st October

Paul said: 'I even found an altar with this inscription: *To an unknown god*. Now what you worship as something unknown I am going to proclaim to you.

Acts 17:23

To so many today, God is unknown. Worship is a mystery – prayer is a foreign language. There is fear for the future, uncertainty about the present and a complete lack of knowledge about God, the Beginning and the End, the Father of our Lord Jesus Christ. And very few people are so keen to know about God that they make their own efforts to find out about Him! Lord, I pray that through the gentle ministering of Christian love and understanding, people will want to know You – to recognise their need to find You, and in the finding long to know You more and more in every aspect of daily life.

> *Me through change and chance He guideth,*
> *Only good and only true.*
> *God unknown, He alone*
> *Calls my heart to be His own.*

Robert Bridges

*   *   *

1st November

To our God and Father be glory for ever and ever.

Philippians 4:20

It's good that the church has a special day for thinking about the band of saints in times past. I'm always amazed by their humility and gentleness and by their living testimony to the strength given by the Holy Spirit. One of the very early saints was tried in about AD 185, and because he would not disown Jesus he was beheaded. The following were among his last words: 'O Lord Jesus Christ, give us a measure of

Thy Spirit that we may be enabled to obey Thy teaching to pacify anger, to moderate desire, to increase love, to put away sorrow... not to be vindictive, not to fear death, ever entrusting our spirit to immortal God, who with Thee and the Holy Ghost liveth and reigneth, world without end.'

> To God be the glory!
> Great things He hath taught us,
> Great things He hath done,
> And great our rejoicing through Jesus the Son.

Frances van Alstyne

*　　*　　*

2nd November

Jesus said, 'And the second [commandment] is... "Love your neighbour as yourself." '

Matthew 22:39

For years I myself have struggled with God's commandment to love others: how could God, I wondered, make such impossible commands?... Scripture readings and sermons on love were quite outside my range of experience: yes, I was aware of God's love for me and I believed I loved Him – but His creatures were another matter altogether... The truth is almost too simple to grasp: 'Anyone who fails to love can never have known God.' It is these words that should be flashed across our TV screens several times a day, because in them lies the real meaning of the word. To know God is to know love, to be touched in that aching void within. How do we know God? By knowing Jesus, by immersing ourselves in His teaching, in prayer, in Scripture and by accepting the gift of God' Spirit.

Delia Smith

Lord, it's not easy, this business of loving people – it's often a hard grind with no reward... Help me not to think of it in this way; help me to look upon everyone I meet during my day through Your light and Your love; help me to find pure, unconditional Love, and to lose myself in it.

*　　*　　*

3rd November

And afterwards,
I will pour our my Spirit on all people.
Your sons and daughters will prophesy,
Your old men will dream dreams,
and your young men will see visions.
Even on my servants, both men and women,
I will pour out my Spirit in those days.
I will show wonders in the heavens and on the earth,
blood and fire and billows of smoke.
The sun will be turned to darkness
and the moon to blood
before the coming of the great and dreadful day of the Lord.
And everyone who calls
on the name of the Lord will be saved; for on Mount Zion and in Jerusalem
there will be deliverance as the Lord has said,
among the survivors
whom the Lord calls.

Joel 2:28–32

*   *   *

4th November

Jesus got up and rebuked the wind and the raging waters;
the storm subsided and all was calm. 'Where is your
faith?' he asked His disciples.

Luke 8:25

But, what is faith? The Bible says, 'It's the evidence of things
unseen.' It is not based on presumption, facile thinking or
credulity. It is rooted in historical events and rests on the
promise of God. It is a growing thing, that reaches forward to
great consequences. When we do not understand, belief is
not easy. But, surely, it is at these times that we have a need
to believe. For faith goes beyond history. It is a personal
commitment, a leap forward. As God continually brings new
enlightenment to our minds and hearts, so our faith can
grow.

Beatrice Hewitt

209

When my love for Christ grows weak,
When for deeper faith I seek,
Then in thought I go to thee
Garden of Gethsemane.

John R. Wreford

*   *   *

5th November

Let nothing move you. Always give yourselves fully to the
work of the Lord, because you know that your labour in
the Lord is not in vain.

1 Corinthians 15:58

We face many perplexing questions today, such as Why does
God permit evil? Why doesn't God intervene and punish
sin? Why does God allow disease? Why does God permit
catastrophe? Yet God's timing is precise! Angel hosts who
witness everything that transpires in our world are not free to
bear up the righteous and deliver the oppressed until God
gives the signal. One day He will. Christ has reminded us
that the wheat and the tares, the righteous and the
unrighteous, are to grow in the field together until the
harvest time when the holy angels gather God's elect and
bring them into His kingdom.

Billy Graham

For the Lord our God shall come
And shall take His harvest home:
From the fields shall in that day
All offences purge away.
Give His angels charge at last
In the fire the tares to cast;
But the fruitful ears to store in His garner evermore.

Henry Alford

*   *   *

6th November

May the God who gives endurance and encouragement
give you a spirit of unity among yourselves as you follow
Jesus Christ, so that with one heart and mouth you may
glorify the God and Father of our Lord Jesus Christ.

Romans 15:5-6

One of the great and enduring prayers of the Christian world
was written by Thomas Cranmer. Born five hundred years
ago, he was a man of devout piety and courageous intellect,
and yet his prayer is so humble: 'Almighty God, Father of
our Lord Jesus Christ, Maker of all things, Judge of all men,
we acknowledge and bewail our manifold sins and
wickedness, which from time to time, we most grievously
have committed, by thought, word and deed... We do
earnestly repent and are heartily sorry for all our misdoings.
Have mercy upon us – forgive us all that is past and grant
that we may ever serve and please Thee in newness of life, to
the honour and glory of Thy name; through Jesus Christ our
Lord. Amen.'

*Jesus... looked towards heaven and prayed: 'Father, the time has come. Glorify your
Son, that Your son may glorify You. For You granted Him authority over all people
that He might give eternal life to all those You have given Him. Now this is eternal
life: that they may know You...'*

John 17:1-3

*　　*　　*

7th November

Jesus said: 'Do not let your hearts be troubled. Trust in
God; trust also in me. In my Father's house are many
rooms... I am going to prepare a place for you.'

John 14:1-2

Yesterday we remembered a man whose memory has
lingered for centuries. Today we read the testimony of a dear

Christian lady. She has never spoken in public, but her loyal attendance at worship and her caring life as wife and mother have been an example of gentleness and love: 'I think the passage of the Bible that has helped me most over the years has been John 14:1–3. I feel that Jesus makes it so clear that although we may meet with many troubles and cares in this world, He is able to give us strength to overcome. I find myself often saying these verses when I am feeling in need of help – in the street, doing my housework or any time, and they always comfort me.

Lord, I pray today for those bearing many cares and burdens... those who have so many problems that they don't know which way to turn. I pray that they, and I, may turn our eyes to Jesus, to trust Him and lean on Him.

* * *

8th November

Jesus said: 'There is nothing concealed that will not be disclosed, or hidden that will not be made known.'

Luke 12:2

On 8th November 1895, quite by accident, one of the greatest medical discoveries was made. Professor Wilhelm Rontgen had left an electric tube on top of a book which just happened to be resting on a photographic plate. Later, when he moved the book, he was amazed and excited to see that a picture of the key which had been inside the book had formed on the photographic plate. His brilliant brain worked overtime! What other substances would allow these 'rays' to pass through them? What about the human body? Rontgen was perplexed by the rays and did not know what to call them, so he chose the name, 'X-rays'. Lord, thank You for such medical advances, and my prayers today are for all who undergo X-ray examination. Calm their fears through the gentleness of understanding staff.

Even the darkness will not be dark to You; the night will shine like the day, for darkness is as light to You. For You created my inmost being; You knit me together in my mother's womb. I praise You because I am fearfully and wonderfully made.

Psalm 139:12–14

* * *

9th November

Jesus said: 'And if anyone gives a cup of cold water to one of these little ones because he is my disciple, I tell you the truth, he will certainly not lose his reward.'

John 10:42

In our society a cup of cold water seems just about the least anyone could give. However, in the hot, arid land in which Jesus lived it was greatly sought after – it was refreshing and a real sign of hospitality. We are all aware that some people tend to get the red carpet treatment because of who they are. But there is no virtue in pandering to a person's position. Jesus specifically mentioned 'little ones' – those who need more care, those perhaps at the back of the queue, those who are overlooked and unimportant by the world's standards. To these, Jesus says, we must be prepared to give the water of life. Lord, help me to give as I need to receive.

You prepare a table before me in the presence of my enemies:
You anoint my head with oil;
My cup overflows.

Psalm 23:5

* * *

10th November

If there is a natural body, there is also a spiritual body. So it is written: 'The first man Adam became a living being'; the last Adam, a life-giving spirit. The spiritual did not come first, but the natural, and after that the spiritual. The first man was of the dust of the earth, the second man

213

was from heaven. As was the earthly man, so are those who are of the earth; and as is the man from heaven, so also are those who are of heaven. And just as we have borne the likeness of the earthly man so shall we bear the likeness of the man from heaven.

I declare to you, brothers, that flesh and blood cannot inherit the kingdom of God, nor does the perishable inherit the imperishable... we will all be changed... For the perishable must clothe itself with the imperishable, and the mortal with immortality.

1 Corinthians 15:44–52

*   *   *

11th November

Defend the cause of the weak and fatherless; maintain the rights of the poor and oppressed. Rescue the weak and needy; deliver them from the hand of the wicked.

Psalm 82:4

Let us never forget, O Lord, the innocent victims of man's inhumanity to man: the millions who were destroyed in the gas chambers and in the holocaust of Hiroshima and Nagasaki, and the few who survived, scarred in mind and body; the uncounted numbers all over the earth who will never have enough to eat, and who, through poverty or ignorance, must watch their children die of hunger; the lepers and the cripples, and the countless others who will live out their lives in illness or disease for which they are given no relief; all who suffer because of their race or their creed or the colour of their skins... Help us, as we go unheedingly about our daily lives, to remember those who silently call to us.

Contemporary American

Lord God of Hosts, be with us yet,
Lest we forget – lest we forget.

Kipling

*   *   *

12th November

Jesus said: 'But I tell you who hear me: Love your
enemies, do good to those who hate you, bless those who
curse you, pray for those who ill-treat you.'

Luke 6:27

Let us all pray for the work of the Bible Society and for the
distribution of Scriptures in prisons. A thirty-four year-old
murderer was converted in a cell at Changi Prison after
reading Luke 6:27–36. Of his feelings before finding Jesus he
wrote: 'In prison I felt alone, hopeless, with no future to look
forward to. I considered committing suicide, but there was
no way to do it in the prison cell. I had no friends, only
enemies. Then two of those enemies became Christians – I
was amazed at the change in their behaviour and I wanted to
get to know this Jesus of theirs. I wanted to read the Bible but
my pride held me back.' His opportunity came when a Bible
fell out of another prisoner's bag onto the floor. The
murderer read and believed: 'After years of sinfulness I felt
peace and joy flooding into me.'

*Jesus said: 'If someone strikes you on one cheek, turn to him the other also... Do to
others as you would have them do to you... Love your enemies, do good to them...
Then your reward will be great, and you will be sons of the Most High, because He is
kind to the ungrateful and wicked.'*

Luke 6:27–35

*   *   *

13th November

'Even to your old age and grey hairs I am He, I am He
who will sustain you. I have made you and I will carry
you.'

Isaiah 46:4

There was a song by the Beatles which included the words,
'will you still love me when I'm sixty-four?' To a teenager,
the age of sixty-four is an eternity away – but for those past

that age, it sounds almost young. For so many the years of ageing are lonely, pain-racked and frustrating. Often the elderly are not given a great deal of thought by the 'fit and busy'. What a comfort it is to know that God's love does not fade, God's concern does not waver: He knows and understands and loves us, whatever our age and condition. God loves us right into His radiant presence and into eternity. Lord, I am Yours; I turn to You and depend upon You. I rest in the knowledge that however difficult the day, You will carry me through.

Lord of all compassion, encircle and shield the old and frail; surround them with Your tender care. Support them when worried by failing powers and increasing infirmity, loss of independence, loss of usefulness, feelings of being a nuisance, fears of illness and fears of death... Thank You that age is no barrier to Your love.

Joy Whyte

* * *

14th November

Jesus said: 'Come to me, all you who are weary and burdened, and I will give you rest. Take my yoke upon you and learn from me...'

Matthew 11:28

Lord, You lift me from the guilt, fear and regret of years, and in its place Your gentle yoke, even when resisted, changes me. I do not understand suffering. In the isolation of Your agony is Your burden eased by acts of love... by sacrificial lives? Is Your burden shared by the suffering of the hungry and the sick? Lord, in spite of my fear... implant in me the courage to make some sacrifice, somewhere in my life, that may lighten, by an infinitessimal fraction, the weight of Your cross.

Frank Topping

Near the cross, O Lamb of God,
Bring its scenes before me;
Help me walk from day to day
With its shadow o'er me.

Frances Jane van Alstyne

* * *

15th November

Jesus said: 'Peace I leave with you; my peace I give you.'

John 14:27

Christ came to preach peace to us who by our nature are at cross-purposes with God. Indeed, He Himself is our peace. This totally new relationship of a man with God comes about, not through man's efforts of achievements, but by God's outgoing love accepted by an unworthy recipient. It is when we reach the point of realizing our utter need that the grace of God can operate and we can enter a new relationship of peace with God. It is in the purpose of God that constantly and all over the world communities should grow up of men and women living in a relationship of peace and love with one another and with Him... Peace with God. Peace in our inter-personal relationships and in our community.

Dr Donald Coggan

Christ is the world's Peace, He and none other;
No one can serve Him and despise his brother.
Who else unites us, one in God the Father?
Glory to God on high.

F. Pratt Green

*   *   *

16th November

In the days to come Jacob will take root, Israel will bud and blossom and fill all the world with fruit.

Isaiah 27:6

I'm always very impressed when friends exhibit their blooms. They have tended them since they were bulbs, kept them cool and moist and brought them out into the sunlight and warmth at just the right time to encourage growth. To me the miracle is that all along the bulb has the capacity to produce a flower – it has been programmed to do just that. Even in seed, the potential for the flower is there.

The promise of God came to a small tribe called the Israelites that one day they would be numberless and scattered throughout the world. Which would have sounded the more absurd in 600 BC – that the Israelites would in the future be living all over the world, or that man would one day walk on the moon? Don't forget that all things are possible with God – and the power of God in your soul can bring out blossoms of love and kindness in a way you would never have imagined. Trust God. We don't work the miracle – He does.

God's flowers – well, they are His thoughts in colours and perfumes... Blest are the pure in heart, for they see God everywhere, in the face of a little child, a dewdrop, a daisy... yes, they see Him everywhere.

Gypsy Smith

* * *

17th November

Love must be sincere. Hate what is evil; cling to what is good. Be devoted to one another in brotherly love. Honour one another above yourselves. Never be lacking in zeal, but keep your spiritual fervour, serving the Lord. Be joyful in hope, patient in affliction, faithful in prayer. Share with God's people who are in need. Practice hospitality.

Bless those who persecute you; bless and do not curse. Rejoice with those who rejoice; mourn with those who mourn. Live in harmony with one another. Do not be proud but be willing to associate with people of low position. Do not be conceited.

Do not repay anyone evil for evil. Be careful to do what is right in the eyes of everybody. If it is possible, as far as it depends on you, live at peace with everyone... Do not be overcome by evil; but overcome evil with good.

Romans 12:9–20

* * *

18th November

> Once more Jesus put his hands on the man's eyes. Then his eyes were opened, his sight was restored, and he saw everything clearly.
>
> Mark 8:22

Not many people are saddled with such a name as Venatius Honorius Clementianus Fortunatus – very possibly his friends gave him a nick-name equivalent to 'Fred'! As a young man he went on a pilgrimage to give thanks for healing from an eye complaint and was prevented from returning home by the war in northern Italy. He wrote poems and hymns, including a volume of hymns for all the Christian festivals in the year – which for the sixth century AD, was amazingly modern.

Lord, give me vision with which to read the writings of the Christian men and women of past centuries, and may I feel at one with the saints on earth and the saints in heaven.

> *Faithful cross, thou sign of triumph,*
> *Now for man the noblest tree:*
> *None in foliage, none in blossom,*
> *None in fruit thy peer may be.*
> *Symbol of the world's redemption*
> *For the weight that hung on thee.*
>
> *Fortunatus (535–600)*

* * *

19th November

> As Jesus was walking beside the sea of Galilee, He saw two brothers, Simon called Peter and his brother Andrew... they were fishermen. 'Come, follow me,' said Jesus. At once they left their nets and followed Him.
>
> Matthew 4:18

He comes to us as One unknown, without a name, as of old by the lakeside He came to those who knew Him not. He speaks to us the same word, 'Follow me' and sets us to the task which He has to fulfil for our time. He commands. And to those who obey Him, whether they be wise or simple, He will reveal Himself in the toils, the conflicts, the sufferings which they shall pass through in His fellowship, and as an ineffable mystery, they shall learn in their own experience who He is.

Albert Schweitzer

O unfamiliar God, we seek You in the places you have already left, and fail to see You even when You stand before us. Grant us so to recognise Your strangeness that we need not cling to our familiar grief, but may be freed to proclaim resurrection in the name of Christ.

Janet Morley

*   *   *

20th November

Stephen, full of the Holy Spirit... said, 'Look, I see heaven open and the Son of Man standing at the right hand of God.'

Acts 7:56

Lord, our Father,
By sending Your only Son into the world You have brought Salvation to us all.
Grant a joyful welcome to Your Gospel from all the peoples of the earth,
That they may praise Your name and rejoice in Your redemption.
Even in these dark and anxious days, when unbelief, violence and
Egotism seem to prevail and hold humanity captive,
Your good news comforts us,
Proclaiming unceasingly that Your redemption is at hand.
You encourage us to vigilance and prayer so that we may stand before
The Son of Man upon the day of His coming...

Waldensian Evangelical Church in Italy

'Behold, I am coming soon! My reward is with me, and I will give to everyone according to what he has done. I am the Alpha and Omega, the First and the Last, the Beginning and

220

the End...' The Spirit and the bride say, 'Come!' And let him who hears say, 'Come!'

Revelation 22:12–13, 17

* * *

21st November

Our holy and glorious temple, where our fathers praised you, has been burned with fire, and all that we treasured lies in ruins!

Isaiah 64:11

The prophet Isaiah was expressing the woes of the Israelites. They believed that God was punishing them for their sin and had turned His back upon them. We can feel their desolation as they groan, 'all that we treasured lies in ruins!' for, at some time, most of us have uttered similar sentiments. We may not necessarily grieve over the destruction of 'glorious temples' – though many churches have indeed fallen into decay and disuse – but so often in our lives our hopes are dashed.

Lord, I'm praying today for those whose marriages lie in ruins... whose health has caved in... who have lost their jobs... lost homes... lost children through accident or illness... lost their partners... Lord, in these inconsolable moments of life be near, be our strength, be love when there are no words to offer.

Do not pray for easy lives.
Pray to be stronger.
Do not pray for tasks equal to your powers.
Pray for powers equal to your tasks.

Philip Brooks

* * *

22nd November

But you are a chosen people, a royal priesthood, a holy
nation, a people belonging to God, that you may declare
the praises of Him who called you out of darkness into
His wonderful light.

1 Peter 2:9

'As one gazes at the vision of beauty and the inspiration of
Michelangelo's Sistine Chapel ceiling, the creation seems
impossible for man to achieve. Yet, born of utter emptiness
and out of an abyss of despair arose light and form and
knowledge. Despair and loneliness are wreathed together in
the "dark night of the soul". Yet, the sun is shining, it is
only that we do not see it'. So wrote Beatrice Hewitt. And
how true that is – there is wonderful light always available
even in our darkest moments... God calls us out of our
darknesses of fear, of illness, of broken hearts; He calls us
into the light of Christ's love. In that warm light may we
learn to live again.

Eternal Light! Eternal Light!
O how shall I whose native sphere is dark,
Whose mind is dim, before the Ineffable appear,
And on my naked spirit bear the uncreated beam?

Thomas Binney

*   *   *

23rd November

Jesus said: 'The kingdom of heaven is like yeast that a
woman took and mixed into a large amount of flour until
it worked through the whole dough.'

Matthew 13:33

Juan Luis Segundo argues that the normal condition of the
church in society is that of a creative minority, as indicated
by the symbolism of leaven. The purpose of leaven, he
suggests, is not to transform the whole piece of dough into

222

leaven, but into bread. So the church is meant to be a transforming ferment in humanity. We find echoes of this thought in the Old Testament teaching of the remnant. And surely, Jesus did not intend His hearers to imagine a clone society of apostles. No, Christians are the salt, the added extra, the remnant, the yeast which helps communities to rise out of littleness and insularity and become vibrant groups of caring individuals. Paradoxically, the yeast only works when it has been kneaded and thoroughly dispersed throughout the dough. Lord, give me the humility to say, 'Use me, Just where and when and how You will.'

> *Lord, endue Thy word from heaven*
> *With such love and light and power,*
> *That in us, its silent leaven*
> *May work on from hour to hour.*

Karl J. P. Spitta

* * *

24th November

Jesus said: 'Watch out that no-one decieves you. For many will come in my name, claiming, "I am the Christ," and will deceive many. You will hear of wars and rumours of wars, but see to it that you are not alarmed. Such things must happen, but the end is still to come. Nation will rise against nation, and kingdom against kingdom. There will be famines and earthquakes in various place. All these are the beginning of birth-pains.

   Then you will be handed over to be persecuted and put to death, and you will be hated by all nations because of me. At that time many will turn away from the faith and will betray and hate each other, and many false prophets will appear and deceive many people. Because of the increase of wickedness, the love of most will grow cold, but he who stands firm to the end will be saved. And this gospel of the kingdom will be preached in the whole world as a testimony to all nations, and then the end will come.

Matthew 24:4–14

* * *

25th November

'I the Lord do not change... Return to me, and I will return to you.'

Malachi 3:6-7

In her long and fascinating life in the Salvation Army, the late Commissioner Catherine Bramwell Booth was always very definite about the importance of 'making a decision'. Bringing people to the point of putting their lives into the hands of Jesus was a great driving force of her work. Her grandmother had been a big influence on her: 'Grandma used to say lots of people came out to the front saying they needed more faith. She said that was a mistake. It wasn't faith they needed, it was the willingness to be obedient to God's commands. That's what they needed. And that is true, I think, today... human nature hasn't changed.'

Lord, I do indeed see that human nature has not changed, and yet I draw comfort from the fact that Your divine nature has not changed either. 'O Safe to the Rock that is higher than I...' I make my decision, Lord, to turn to You... 'Thou blest Rock of Ages, I'm hiding in Thee.'

*   *   *

26th November

Woe to you who are complacent... You drink wine by the bowlful and use the finest lotions, but you do not grieve over the ruin of Joseph.

Amos 6:1, 6

Complacency! 'I'm alright, Jack!' We see complacency around us, and we tend to think that it is a twentieth-century vice. How Satan can deceive us... Complacency is one of his best weapons! The prophet Amos gave a vivid description of the life of the wealthy, and it was surprisingly modern. With only a few adjustments, it could have been written yesterday. The prophet's words got straight to the point. Jesus, the greatest prophet, had stinging things to say to the complacent. Never once did Jesus hint that His followers need not worry about others because they had brought calamity upon themselves. He did not stipulate restrictions and limitations to compassion. He said, 'Feed my lambs', 'Love your neighbour as yourself', 'In as much as you do this for the least of your brothers, you do it for me'. Am I hearing Your words, Lord, or am I too self-satisfied and complacent?

> O brother man, fold to thy heart they brother –
> Where pity dwells, the peace of God is there.
> To worship rightly is to love each other,
> Each smile a hymn, each kindly deed a prayer.
>
> *John G. Whittier*

* * *

27th November

'Can you fathom the mysteries of God? Can you probe the limits of the Almighty?'

Job 11:7

> *Can we by searching find out God or formulate His ways?*
> *Can numbers measure what He is or words contain His praise?*
>
> *Although His being is too bright for human eyes to scan,*
> *His meaning lights our shadowed world through Christ, the Son of Man.*
>
> *Our boastfulness is turned to shame, our profit counts as loss,*
> *When earthly values stand beside the manger and the cross.*
>
> *We there may recognise His light, may kindle in its rays*
> *Find there the source of penitence, the starting-point for praise.*
>
> *There God breaks in upon our search, makes birth and death His own,*
> *He speaks to us in human terms to make His glory known.*
>
> *Elizabeth Cosnett*

Oh, the depths of the riches of the wisdom and knowledge of God! How unsearchable His judgements, and His paths

beyond tracing out! Who has known the mind of the Lord?...
For from Him and through Him and to Him we are all
things. To Him be the glory for ever. Amen.

Romans 11:33-36

*   *   *

28th November

And hope does not disappoint us, because God has
poured out His love into our hearts by the Holy Spirit,
whom He has given us.

Romans 5:5

The approaching season of Advent is a time of hope. Yet
somehow it seems that once Christmas is passed our hopes
collapse and we feel disappointed by events... So what goes
wrong? Paul tells us that hope itself does not disappoint, so it
must be human weakness – our selfishness, covetousness,
poor temper... all the things that hinder the influence of
God's Holy Spirit. When self talks, nothing else is heard.

Lord, You bring me to my knees so that I will realise that
human weakness has always got in the way, dashing the
hopes of people, both young and old, down through the
centuries. We are all equally at fault, equally in need. May
our hopes now be centred on Jesus, the hope of the world.

The hopes and fears of all the years are met in Thee...

Phillip Brooks

*   *   *

29th November

Hear the word of the Lord... 'The multitude of your
sacrifices – what are they to me?' says the Lord... 'Stop
bringing meaningless offerings!'

Isaiah 1:10, 13

Another month and Christmas will be over! A month of enforced jollity and frantic preparations... sacrifices on the altar of consumerism... Lord, I feel I've had enough already, so I can just imagine how sick you must be to see the birth of Jesus mocked by this ritual, festive jamboree. Before it is too late I pray for simplicity of mind and heart, so that I may approach this season of Advent in true and worshipful preparation... I want to see beyond the tinsel and razamataz to a bare stable, to the life of a man without material possessions, to a death on a bare cross... Prepare my heart for seeing Jesus in the poverty of today.

> *In Bethlehem's home was there found no room*
> *For Thy holy nativity:*
> *O come to my heart, Lord Jesus,*
> *There is room in my heart for Thee.*

Emily E. S. Elliott

*   *   *

30th November

Jesus said: 'When a man believes in me, he does not believe in me only, but in the one who sent me. When he looks at me he sees the one who sent me.'

John 12:44–45

Grant to us, O God, the seeing eye, the hearing ear, the understanding mind and the loving heart, so that we may see your glory, and hear your word, and understand your truth and answer to your love. Grant that these few minutes with you may send us into the world again more kind to others; more honest with ourselves; more loyal to you, through Jesus Christ our Lord. Amen.

Dr William Barclay

> *Open our eyes, Lord, we want to see Jesus,*
> *To reach out and touch Him,*
> *And say that we love Him:*

Open our ears, Lord, and help us to listen,
O Open our eyes, Lord, we want to see Jesus.

Robert Cure

*   *   *

1st December

A shoot will come up from the stump of Jesse;
from his roots a Branch will bear fruit.
The Spirit of the Lord will rest on him –
the Spirit of wisdom and understanding,
the Spirit of counsel and of power,
the Spirit of knowledge and the fear of the Lord –
and he will delight in the fear of the Lord.
He will not judge by what he sees with his eyes,
or decide by what he hears with his ears;
but with righteousness he will judge the needy,
with justice he will give decisions for the poor of the earth...
Righteousness will be his belt
and faithfulness the sash round his waist.
The wolf will live with the lamb,
the leopard will lie down with the goat,
the calf and the lion and the yearling together;
and a little child will lead them...
For the earth will be full of the knowledge of the Lord.

Isaiah 11:1-6, 9

*   *   *

2nd December

He will reign on David's throne and over his kingdom,
establishing and upholding it with justice and righteousness from that time on and for ever.

Isaiah 9:7

Beyond the darkness, there is light.
Beyond the griefs and pains of the moment is the promise of
food and freedom for all.
Beyond our current distress is the dream of a tapestry

through which is woven the rainbow colours of truth, freedom, peace and love.
And in the centre of this tapestry is the Son of God who became human to uphold the Kingdom of justice and righteousness.

Karl Gaspar (Philippines)

His power increasing still shall spread,
His reign no end shall know;
Justice shall guard His throne above
And peace abound below.

John Morison

* * *

3rd December

'So there is hope for your future,' declares the Lord.

Jeremiah 31:17

Advent is a time of expectation, of hope – and how much we need hope at the moment. The church's hope in this season is a rich, multi-layered concept. It is hope for the coming of the Lord in glory, when all that is wrong in the world will be made right. And it is hope for the coming of the Lord in humility, when our hard hearts will melt before the sun. Human hopes have so often been dashed to the ground or twisted. Human beings are continually disillusioned... Yet hope, like cheerfulness, keeps breaking in. This hope is no illusion. For there is something to look forward to; and for this future, God's future, we were made.

Bishop Richard Harries

Come then, let us hasten yonder;
Here let all, great and small,
Kneel in awe and wonder;
Love Him who with Love is yearning –
Hail the star that from afar
Bright with hope is burning.

Paul Gerhardt

* * *

4th December

I thank my God every time I remember you. In all my prayers for all of you, I always pray with joy because of your partnership in the gospel...

Philippians 1:3-4

The Baptist minister and hymn writer John Fawcett was invited to work in a prestigious church in the city of London. He was tempted to accept – but at the last moment he decided that he could not leave his country friends. Friendship is a rare and wonderful blessing. These are verses from one of his compositions, which we can think of as a hymn to friendship:

> Blest be the tie that binds our hearts in Christian love:
> The fellowship of kindred minds is like to that above.
>
> We share our mutual woes, our mutual burdens bear;
> And often for each other flows the sympathizing tear.
>
> When for a while we part, this thought will soothe our pain,
> That we shall still be joined in heart and one day meet again.

Dear Lord, who enjoyed the friendship of the twelve disciples, and that of Mary, Martha, Lazarus and so many more, I thank You for my friends... I want to spend a few moments now in remembering those who feel friendless today... May they come to know that they have a friend in Jesus.

*   *   *

5th December

She wrapped Him in strips of cloth and placed Him in a manger, because there was no room for them in the inn.

Luke 2:7

Trevor Huddleston lived for years in Johannesburg in Africa. One day in Sophiatown a violent storm tore the roofs off the corrugated iron shacks in which the black people lived. Some of the men took Huddleston to see their plight. 'I went with them to see for myself, and I found a woman in labour amongst those around the brazier, and her baby was born under the winter stars that night. There was no room for them at the inn – and so, on a winter night in Bethlehem nearly two thousand years ago, the Son of God had entered the world in the bleak and barren shelter of a stable... I think that the carols, beautiful as they are, of our day, can distort the truth: can be a dangerous escape from the realities of the Christian faith if we do not remember that, in fact, God's entry into the world was unwelcomed and uncared for when it happened.'

The true light that gives light to every man was coming to the world. He was in the world, and though the world was made through Him, the world did not recognise Him. He came to that which was His own, but His own did not receive Him.

John 1:9–11

*   *   *

6th December

And we have seen and testify that the Father has sent His
Son to be the Saviour of the world.

1 John 4:14

Our Father up in heaven long, long years ago,
Looked down in His great mercy upon the earth below
And saw that folks were lonely and lost in deep despair,
And so He said, 'I'll send my Son to walk among them there...
So they can hear Him speaking and feel His nearness too,
And see the many miracles that Faith alone can do...
For, if man really sees Him and can touch His healing hand,
I know it will be easier to believe and understand.'
And so the Holy Christ child came down to live on earth,
And that is why we celebrate His Holy, wondrous birth;
And that is why at Christmas the world becomes aware
That heaven may seem far away
           BUT
      God is Everywhere!

Helen Steiner Rice

O Lord, my God, my loving heavenly Father, I pray for the pure joy of the realization that truly Jesus, the Saviour of the world, has been born.

* * *

7th December

I urge, then, first of all, that requests, prayers, intercession and thanksgiving be made for everyone...

1 Timothy 2:1

We all like to receive cards at Christmas – they show that our friends and relatives have remembered us, that they care about us. However, it means much more to be remembered by name before God in prayer. Lord, I pray for those who have no family to cherish as this very family-centred season approaches. I pray for families separated by distance... Through the bonding of prayer may they feel closer to one another, and may they be drawn closer to the Saviour's side. Forgive me that my prayers are so short, so one-sided, so lacking in expressions of thankfulness... Lord, teach me to turn to You with words and with soft silences, bearing the needs before You and trusting in Your mercy...

How little we realise the great importance of intercessory prayer. If at this moment you pray for someone, even though he is on the other side of the globe, the hand of Jesus will touch him.

Corrie ten Boom

* * *

8th December

In the sixth month, God sent the angel Gabriel to Nazareth, a town in Galilee, to a virgin pledged to be married to a man named Joseph, a descendant of David. The virgin's name was Mary. The angel went to her and said, 'Greetings, you who are highly favoured! The Lord is with you.'

Mary was greatly troubled at his words and wondered what kind of greeting this might be. But the angel said to her, 'Do not be afraid, Mary, you have found favour with God. You will be with child and give birth to a son, and you are to give him the name Jesus. He will be great and will be called the Son of the Most High. The Lord God will give him the throne of his father David, and he will reign over the house of Jacob for ever; his kingdom will never end... The Holy Spirit will come upon you and the power of the Most High will overshadow you. So the holy one to be born will be called the Son of God.'

Luke 1:26–35

*   *   *

9th December

And on that day they offered great sacrifices, rejoicing because God had given them great joy... the sound of rejoicing could be heard far away.'

Nehemiah 12:43

We rejoice this Christmas – but not everyone can rejoice. Some have no cause for rejoicing. They may even not be glad that they are alive; they may prefer to be dead rather than hungry, heartbroken or homeless. In many parts of the world refugees live in an emotional vacuum... In Africa there is famine and a desperate need for many types of nutritional and technological aid. In our society, where there is such great hunger for material possessions, I pray for those who hunger for someone to care for them... Lord, the Light and Joy of all mankind, kindle our hearts to spread the sound of our rejoicing into all the needy corners of our community, for the sake of Jesus Christ, the Joy of Bethlehem.

Rejoice, O people, in this living hour:
Low lies our pride and human wisdom dies;
But on the Cross God's love reveals His power,

And from His waiting church new hopes arise.
Rejoice that while our sinfulness divides,
One Christian fellowship of love abides.

Albert Bayly

*　　*　　*

10th December

Jesus said: 'If you hold to my teaching, you are really my disciples. Then you will know the truth, and the truth will set you free.'

John 8:32

Freedom seems to be an intangible commodity that is only precious to people if they don't have it. Jesus lived amongst a people whose land was occupied by a foreign power. The Jews longed to be freed from Roman rule; Jesus understood what freedom meant to them. On 10th December 1964 the Nobel Peace Prize was awarded to Dr Martin Luther King, who was waging a non-violent crusade to gain freedom and equality for his people. Lord, I cannot imagine the desperation which makes people dedicate their entire lives to gain freedom and justice – forgive me. Forgive my apathy – I cannot grasp the urgency of the need to know Your truth. I so lightly listen to the truth that can make me free; I set so little value on the priceless freedom of the Spirit. Lord, help me to understand.

When we allow freedom to ring from every town and every hamlet... we will be able to speed up that day when all of God's children, black men and white men, Jews and Gentiles, Protestants and Catholics, will be able to join hands and sing: 'Free at last! Great God Almighty, we are free at last!'

Martin Luther King

*　　*　　*

234

11th December

Then Peter said [to the crippled man], 'Silver or gold I do
not have, but what I have I give you. In the name of Jesus
Christ of Nazareth, walk!'

Acts 3:6

It's not the things that can be bought
*   that are life's richest treasure.*
It's just the little heart-gifts that money cannot measure...
A cheerful smile, a friendly word, a sympathetic nod
Are priceless little treasures from the storehouse of our God.
They are the things that can't be bought
*   with silver or with gold,*
For thoughtfulness and kindness and love are never sold...
They are the priceless things in life
*   for which no one can pay,*
And the giver finds rich recompense in giving them away.
Helen Steiner Rice

I Thank You, Lord, from the depth of my being for the
priceless gifts and blessings which have been given me...
From the storehouse of Your love in my heart may I too give
and give and give again...

*   *   *

12th December

Listen! I tell you a mystery...

1 Corinthians 15:51

However sophisticated mankind becomes, the wonder and
mystery of a birth never fails to give us a special thrill. Our
thoughts turn at this time of year to a baby's cry in
Bethlehem – a whisper of sound echoing down the centuries
to modern supermarkets, tenement blocks, villages,
penthouse flats and suburban streets... We celebrate the
greatest mystery of all time – God Himself being born in
order to give the one definitive example of how we should

235

live together in peace and wholeness, in true *Shalom*. Amidst all the preparation and fun of this Advent season, let's take time to find God and let the mystery of Christmas speak to us. God cares about us – cares about you – and through Jesus Christ He has reached out in His love.

> *Light from a stained glass window –*
> *Peals from an ancient spire,*
> *A crib in a special corner, carols from the choir:*
> *The mysteries of whispered prayers quietly ascend above*
> *To God, who sent a Baby, to bless us with His love.*

Edwin Jukes

*   *   *

13th December

No-one has ever seen God; but if we love each other, God lives in us and His love is made complete in us.

1 John 4:12

In their book of prayers, Michael Hollings and Etta Gullick write of the wonder of God's love: 'You have done so much for me, loved me so much. I wish I loved you more and could show it. What can I say or do? When I feel your love, it is as though I would burst into laughter and achieve anything for you or anyone else. It can pass all too quickly, and in fact I don't live up to what I want to do for you. But it is wonderful all the same, this strength and power, this serenity, this depth. Even when I fail your love, your love doesn't fail me. Oh, for an unshakable love like yours, which would go out from me to you and to all those I find so hard to love who are round about me.'

> *Thine am I by all ties:*
> *By Thine own cords of love*
> *So sweetly wound around me,*
> *I to Thee am closely bound.*

Charles E. Mudie

*   *   *

14th December

Joseph went to Bethlehem to register with Mary, who was pledged to be married to him and was expecting a child.

Luke 2:5

Laughter and love and the delighted surprise of totally unexpected joy; these are not merely the trappings of Christmas, but the very substance of its meaning. God calls us to savour these experiences, to open ourselves to them, and let them fill our souls. This is not in denial of the world's pain and sorrow, but in the knowledge that such experiences are the instruments that equip us for creative confrontation with life, as they overflow into lives around us, to combat sorrow, suffering and death. Let us prepare ourselves to live the Christmas event.

Fredrick A. Styles

How silently, how silently,
The wondrous gift is given!
So God imparts to human hearts
The blessings of His Heaven.
No ear may hear His coming, but in this world of sin,
Where meek souls will receive Him, still the dear Christ enters in.

Phillipa Brooks

*   *   *

15th December

This is how the birth of Jesus Christ came about. His mother Mary was pledged to be married to Joseph, but before they came together, she was found to be with child through the Holy Spirit. Because Joseph her husband was a righteous man and did not want to expose her to public disgrace, he had in mind to divorce her quietly.

But after he had considered this, an angel of the Lord appeared to him in a dream and said, 'Joseph, son of David, do not be afraid to take Mary home as your wife, because what is conceived in her is from the Holy Spirit.

She will give birth to a son, and you are to give him the name Jesus, because he will save his people from their sins.'

All this took place to fulfil what the Lord had said through the prophet. 'The virgin will be with child and will give birth to a son, and they will call him Immanuel' – which means 'God with us'.

When Joseph woke up, he did what the angel of the Lord had commanded him and took Mary home as his wife.

Matthew 1:18–24

*　　*　　*

16th December

He came to that which was His own, but His own did not receive Him. Yet to all who received Him, He gave the right to become children of God...

John 1:11

There is a legend about a holy man who gave up wealth and position to live in prayer and simplicity in the forest. One day some townspeople asked him to come and pray in a church which they had just rebuilt. When he reached the door he stopped. 'I'm sorry,' he said, 'there's no room, I can't get in.' 'What do you mean?' they asked. 'There's a place reserved for you at the front.' He replied, 'I'll never get as far as that. The building is crammed full of ideas and words and plans. Make some space to receive God, and then I will come back and pray with you.'

Angela Ashwin

Dear Lord, I am so guilty of being full of ideas – my ideas... Words tumble from my mouth about anything and everything except Your love and guidance in my life... I make my plans to suit myself. Lord, help me to receive Your word of truth and grace – here and now.

*　　*　　*

17th December

And God said, 'Let there be Light,' and there was Light.
God saw that the Light was good...

Genesis 1:3

> *One day, God said, 'Let there be Love.'*
> *And a child was born whose name was Light.*
> *'I am the Light of the world,' he said.*
> *'If you follow me you shall not walk in darkness.'*
> *By the Light humanity was liberated,*
> *The blind received sight*
> *And to the poor the Good News came.*
>
> *Today, God says, 'Let there be hope,'*
> *Beholding the rainbow of covenant*
> *Suspended from the cross to the empty tomb.*
> *The Light of the dawn is here*
> *Giving hope to all.*
>
> *Today we celebrate the Light, celebrate the hope.*
> *In unity and in diversity,*
> *Because of the Light, the Cross, and the Heart,*
> *For the shalom of the world.*
> *Together we build the future in hope.*

Hae-Jong Kim

Lord, bring to my soul the realisation that Life, Light and
Joy are found in Your presence, through Jesus Christ, the
Light of the world.

*   *   *

18th December

Jesus said: 'I am the Light of the world. Whoever follows
me will never walk in darkness, but will have the light of
life.'

John 8:12

Helen Keller, who was blind and deaf from infancy, said: 'I believe that God is in me as the sun is in the colour and fragrance of a flower – the Light of my darkness, the Voice in my silence.' As I meditate on those profoundly moving words from someone whose early life must have been sheer hell, I realise how little we understand of what goes on in the hearts and minds of those who are handicapped in mind or body. Some lie today in hospital beds, in comas, beyond the reach of medicine – but not beyond the reach of the Light of Eternal Love. I believe that You, Lord, are in each life – in the life of the premature feotus, the sick child, the terminally ill teenager, the crash victim, the sufferer of senile dementia... Lord, be to each one their Light, and by Your reflected Light comfort those who love them.

> Brightest and best of the sons of the morning,
> Dawn on our darkness and lend us Thine aid;
> Star of the east, the horizon adorning,
> Guide where our infant Redeemer is laid.

Reginald Heber

*　　*　　*

19th December

So they [the shepherds] hurried off and found Mary and Joseph, and the baby who was lying in the manger.

Luke 2:16

Notice in our Nativity scene that at the heart of the people gathered is a family. We shall probably never be able to calculate the influence that this aspect of the Christmas story has had on history. Enough to say that still today Christmas is a family time... In blessing Mary and Joseph through being part of their family it seems to me God made it easy for us to believe that He desires to bless all families with His presence. Christmas is God's way of setting a new value on people – it also expresses His special place and regard for the family, for He joined the human race within the family unit, and now we see a new place given to childhood.

Jeffrey Sharp

Angels sing again the song you sang,
Bring God's glory to the heart of man;
Sing that Bethlem's little baby can
Be salvation to the soul.

Michael Perry

*　　*　　*

20th December

The Lord said to me, 'My grace is sufficient for you, for
my power is made perfect in weakness.'

2 Corinthians 12:9

The central figure of every nativity scene is the ultimate in
weakness – a human baby, the most frail and vulnerable of
all new life in creation. Yet God gave us His perfect gift in
just this form. As we grow physically, it's easy to forget how
dependent we once were – until something happens to bring
us face to face with the reality of our weakness at any age –
physical, mental and spiritual. And into our moments of
deep crisis the Lord speaks. Only when we acknowledge our
frailty and need of Him can He console us by His grace and
power.

Lord, hear my prayer. I put aside the carols, the children's
excitement, the glitz and sparkle of man-made Christmas. I
need You more than ever before at the centre of my life.

Frail children of dust – and feeble as frail,
In Thee do we trust,
Nor find Thee to fail.

Robert Grant

*　　*　　*

21st December

Jesus said, 'I tell you that there is more rejoicing in
heaven over one sinner who repents than over ninety-nine
righteous persons...'

Luke 15:7

241

Unemployed and homeless, Dave was a stranger in the city. It didn't occur to him to go to a church on Christmas Day, so he huddled in a glass-sided shelter on the seafront. Cold and alone, he was found that night by a volunteer group from a local church on their weekly 'soup-run'. After giving him soup and turkey sandwiches, they phoned around, found him a bed in a men's hostel and delivered him with an extra blanket to the door. During the short journey they simply told Dave that for them Christmas meant remembering those who still 'found no room at the inn'. Jesus came to a world that had no room for Him, and yet He lived to seek and to save the lost. It was He who had led the soup-run group to Dave that night.

Lord, in the midst of affluence, I pray today for the work of the Salvation Army and of the churches that open their doors to give Christmas meals and friendship to the lonely and to those who cannot help themselves... May I learn the holy joy that only comes by giving to others.

*   *   *

22nd December

And there were shepherds living out in the fields near by, keeping watch over their flocks at night. An angel of the Lord appeared to them and the glory of the Lord shone around them, and they were terrified. But the angel said to them, 'Do not be afraid. I bring you good news of great joy that will be for all people. Today in the town of David a Saviour has been born to you; He is Christ the Lord. This will be a sign to you: You will find a baby wrapped in strips of cloth and lying in a manger.'

Suddenly a great company of the heavenly host appeared with the angel, praising God and saying, 'Glory to God in the highest, and on earth peace to men on whom his favour rests.'

When the angels had left them, and gone into heaven, the shepherds said to one another, 'Let's go to Bethlehem and see this thing that has happened, which the Lord has told us about.'

So they hurried off and found Mary and Joseph, and
the baby, who was lying in the manger.

Luke 2:8–16

*   *   *

23rd December

And he will be called Wonderful Counsellor, Mighty
God, Everlasting Father, Prince of Peace.

Isaiah 9:6

Christmas! The star points out the way
   leading to a child
Who has just been born,
Light in the darkness, God with us.
Christmas! Light is shining through the
   dividing walls we have built
Between heaven and earth, men and women,
Old and young, rich and poor,
North and South, East and West;
Light which warms our hearts, brightens our eyes
And melts our icy indifference,
   prejudice and hate,
Just as the wax of the candle melts for
   the flame to burn and glow,
The flame of life, the flame of unity,
   the flame of Peace!

Christian Conference of Asia

O Lord, it is my urgent prayer that the flame of Peace should
burn and glow in my heart. May the warmth and assurance
of a loving and peaceful home shine out the neighbourhood
for those who need You so much.

*   *   *

24th December

But you, Bethlehem Ephrathah, though you are small
among the clans of Judah, out of you will come for me one
who will be ruler over Israel.

Micah 5:2

243

Bethlehem wrapt in night.
Old lamps glow like burnished gold,
Yet somehow hearts of men are cold:
'No room!' they cry, and close each door,
'No room! No room! No room for more.'
The just may feel some guilt, some sad remorse,
'Tis pity vainly spilt, it never changed the course
Of cruel earth or evil men;
It does not now – it did not then...

Once again let Christmas night
Fill your hearts with new delight.
Forget the tinsel, lights and mirth,
Pause to hail the Saviour's birth.
May your thoughts transport you far,
Be wise, and follow still the star:
Sift the gold from all the dross –
Beyond the stable stands a Cross.

Edwin Jukes

At a specific time and at a specific place a specific Person was born and that Person was God of very God, the Lord Jesus Christ. God became personal in Bethlehem.

Billy Graham

*   *   *

25th December

She wrapped Him in strips of cloth and placed Him in a manger.

Luke 2:7

I had been warned that Bethlehem was commercialised. I had been told that after two thousand years it was impossible to be certain of the location of the actual manger. But as I stood looking at the rough stone manger carved from the massive rock beneath the Church of the Holy Nativity in Bethlehem, I felt that these things did not matter. The manger reminded me of the stone trough into which I'd thrown cow cake for my two cows so many years before... it was so ordinary... so natural. Our group paused to sing the

244

simple carol, *Away in a Manger*. This Christmas Day will be the more real for me because I glimpsed an actual place where a baby could have been placed out of harm's way amid the press of people and animals. The cash registers and the gaudy Christmas decorations can never obliterate the simple and miraculous truth of Jesus' birth. In a manger... a baby... my Lord.

> *Away in a manger, no crib for a bed,*
> *The little Lord Jesus laid down His sweet head.*
> *The stars in the bright sky looked down where He lay,*
> *The little Lord Jesus asleep on the hay.*

Anon

* * *

26th December

Jesus said to the servants, 'Fill the jars with water,' so they filled them to the brim. Then He told them, 'Now draw some out and take it to the master of the banquet.'

John 2:7

Luke records in the Acts of the Apostles that the disciple Peter told the crowds that Jesus of Nazareth 'was a man accredited by God to you by miracles, wonder and signs, which God did among you through Him'. I liken Jesus' first miracle in John's Gospel to the annual miracle of Christmas. Somehow the very ordinary becomes special, and the heart that trusts in Him receives a blessing which far exceeds its need or expectation. I saw a plaque in the Holy Land which read: 'Cana proclaims to us that Jesus is the Lord Almighty who turns water into wine, who can still today, by one word, transform anything – sorrow into joy, mountains of difficulty into straight paths.' Do we bring our needs to Him?

> *A lasting gift Jesus gave His own –*
> *To share His bread, His loving cup;*
> *Whatever burdens may bow us down,*
> *He, by His cross, shall lift us up.*

F. Pratt Green

* * *

27th December

From this time many of His disciples turned back and no longer followed Him.

John 6:66

After the candlelit services, after the merry carol singing, after all the excitement of nativities performed by eager and not-so-eager little ones, the Christmas things get put away. Sadly, this is symbolic of how Jesus is treated by many. He is put back in the cupboard until next year. Lord, forgive me if that is what I have begun to do already – if my spirit is flagging with post-Christmas anticlimax. Help me to understand that Your coming to this world is not over and done with. Lord Jesus Christ, Babe of Bethlehem, grow in me... never leave me... In the gift of Your eternal love I find the renewal of my soul. I cannot turn back from Bethlehem. I will follow You each day of my life, closer and ever closer.

Enter then, O Christ most Holy,
Make a Christmas in my heart;
Make a heaven of my manger –
It is heaven where Thou art.

George S. Rowe

* * *

28th December

Jesus said... 'If your eyes are bad, your whole body will be full of darkness. If then the light within you is darkness, how great is that darkness!'

John 6:23

The fireplace that decorates our den at Christmas is a cheerful fake painted to look like brick. Inside a revolving tin disk over a red bulb gives a fleeting illusion of moving flames. The whole effect is so pretty that the fireplace is the focal point of the room. Often people coming in from the cold move to it instinctively, holding out their hands for warmth. But, it is an illusion. It gives no warmth, no comfort. We tend to build our lives around illusions – money, power, social status. How pleasant they are! What fun to have! But, when chilled and bewildered by the dark night of sorrow, we hold out our hands to these things and they are revealed as the illusions they are – with no light, no warmth and no comfort to give.

Ruth Bruns (New Orleans)

Dear Lord, teach us to keep the things of this world in proper perspective, so that we may focus our lives on what is real and enduring.

*   *   *

29th December

Now there was a man in Jerusalem called Simeon, who was righteous and devout. He was waiting for the consolation of Israel, and the Holy Spirit was upon him. It had been revealed to him that he would not die before he had seen the Lord's Christ. Moved by the Spirit, he went into the temple courts. When the parents brought in the child Jesus to do for Him what the custom of the Law required, Simeon took Him in his arms and praised God, saying:

> *'Sovereign Lord, as You have promised,*
> *You now dismiss Your servant in peace.*
> *For my eyes have seen Your salvation,*
> *which You have prepared in the sight of all people,*
> *a light for revelation to the Gentiles*
> *and for glory to Your people of Israel.'*

The child's father and mother marvelled at what was said about Him. Then Simeon blessed them and said to Mary, His mother: 'This child is destined to cause the falling and rising of many in Israel, and to be a sign that will be spoken against, so that the thoughts of many hearts will be revealed. And a sword will pierce your own soul too.'

Luke 2:25–35

*   *   *

30th December

In Him was life, and that life was the light of men. The
light shines in the darkness, but the darkness has not
understood it.

John 1:4–5

You know sometimes how one goes to see a church which one
is told has magnificent windows – and seen from outside they
all look alike, dull, thick and grubby... Then we open the
door and go inside – leave the outer world, enter the inner
world – and the universal light floods through the windows
and bathes us in their colour and beauty and significance,
shows us things of which we had never dreamed, a loveliness
that lies beyond the fringe of speech. And so, in the same
way, we cannot realise God and all our Lord's lovely
meaning as a revelation of God and His eternal Truth and
Beauty, from outside... It is from within the place of prayer,
recollection, worship and love, that we fully and truly receive
the revelation which is made through Christ.

Evelyn Underhill

*Lord, as this year draws to its close I give You thanks for the glimpses which I have
had of Your universal light. May my life be so bathed in colour and the gentle beauty
of Your Spirit that I will meet the new year with joyous prayer and humble worship.*

*   *   *

31st December

That which was from the beginning, which we have
heard, which we have seen with our eyes, which we have
looked at and our hands have touched – this we proclaim
concerning the Word of life.

1 John 1:1

We can't help ourselves – the end of the year sees us all
peering back over what has been – the moments that have
made our hearts soar with joy, the words that we would give

248

a thousand worlds never to have uttered, the anxieties and the hot, streaming tears... life. One whole year of life! Nothing lasts for ever, neither the good nor the bad, not even our looking back.

Lord, as this year closes, I give You thanks for what I have experienced, and I praise You for the things I have seen and heard which enrich my faith for today and give me hope for the future. Yes – nothing lasts for ever except the Word of life made flesh, the indescribable power of the Trinity – Father, Son and Holy Spirit, Alpha and the Omega... into Eternity.

> *Yesterday, today, for ever,*
> *Jesus is the same:*
> *All may change but Jesus never –*
> *Glory to His name!*

*   *   *